As one of the world's longest established
and best-known travel brands,
Thomas Cook are the experts in travel.

For more than 135 years our
guidebooks have unlocked the secrets
of destinations around the world,
sharing with travellers a wealth of
experience and a passion for travel.

**Rely on Thomas Cook as your
travelling companion on your next trip
and benefit from our unique heritage.**

Thomas Cook **pocket** guides

# BILBAO

Your travelling companion since 1873

**Written by Patrick McConnell**
**Updated by Nick Inman & Clara Villanueva**

**Published by Thomas Cook Publishing**
A division of Thomas Cook Tour Operations Limited
Company registration no. 3772199 England
The Thomas Cook Business Park, 9 Coningsby Road,
Peterborough PE3 8SB, United Kingdom
Email: sales@thomascook.com, Tel: +44 (0) 1733 416477
www.thomascookpublishing.com

**Produced by Cambridge Publishing Management Limited**
Burr Elm Court, Main Street, Caldecote CB23 7NU
www.cambridgepm.co.uk

ISBN: 978-1-84848-348-4

© 2006, 2008 Thomas Cook Publishing
This third edition © 2011
Text © Thomas Cook Publishing
Maps © Thomas Cook Publishing/PCGraphics (UK) Limited
Transport map © Communicarta Limited

Series Editor: Karen Beaulah
Production/DTP: Steven Collins

Printed and bound in Spain by GraphyCems

Cover photography © Art Kowalsky/Alamy

# CONTENTS

## SYMBOLS KEY

The following symbols are used throughout this book:

**ⓐ** address  **ⓣ** telephone  **ⓕ** fax  **ⓦ** website address  **ⓔ** email
**ⓛ** opening times  **ⓝ** public transport connections  **ⓘ** important

The following symbols are used on the maps:

| | | | |
|---|---|---|---|
| **ⓘ** | information office | ▪ | point of interest |
| **✈** | airport | O | city |
| **✚** | hospital | O | large town |
| **ⓤ** | police station | ○ | small town |
| **⊟** | bus station | ═ | motorway |
| **⊜** | railway station | — | main road |
| **Ⓜ** | metro | — | minor road |
| **✝** | cathedral | — | railway |
| **❶** | numbers denote featured cafés & restaurants | | |

Hotels and restaurants are graded by approximate price as follows:
**£** budget price  **££** mid-range price  **£££** expensive

Abbreviations used in addresses:
C/ (Calle)
Pl. (Plaza)
Av. (Avenida)

**❿** *The Guggenheim is the icon of modern Bilbao*

INTRODUCING
Bilbao

# Introduction

The city of Bilbao, proud bastion of the Basque way of life, has witnessed a major cultural renaissance. It has much to offer the discerning traveller: history, art, architecture, fine cuisine, lifestyle, shopping, and easy access to fishing villages, beaches and natural parks. The construction of the famous Guggenheim Museum, among other regeneration projects, lifted the city's image into the top rank of European cities. Set on the Mar Cantábrico, or Bay of Biscay, Spain's eighth-largest city has risen to the challenge of overcoming its legacy of industrialisation and pollution – so much so that it has become a model of regeneration for other cities.

The reasons for visiting this Basque city and its surroundings are as varied as they are plentiful. The city's top cultural establishments, the foremost being of course the Guggenheim, are considered European highlights, and the newer, dynamic areas like the Ensanche provide a contrast to the atmospheric historic centre, with its web of ancient streets.

Bilbao is also a handy base for visits to the countryside and natural parks, and provides easy access to the coastal city of San Sebastián, justly considered one of Spain's loveliest places, and quiet, charming Vitoria, seat of the Basque government. The magnificent coastline of the Costa Vasca offers rewards for those who venture out of Bilbao, with fishing villages like Hondarriba and Elantxobe, and beautiful bays such as Bahía de la Concha. In addition, the Bay of Biscay offers numerous fine beaches, from the resort of Getxo along the coast to Lekeiteo and beyond.

The Basque Country, Euskadi to the natives, remains in many parts an unspoiled region, despite the historical development of industry on the peninsula. Rural traditions are well preserved and are an important element of the Basque way of life. The economic recession has been arrested by major urban renewal and the pollution of the Río Nervión is now taken more seriously. The airport and metro gave the city a fresh start with this regeneration. Bilbao is increasingly popular with visitors and the word is out, so get in and explore it while it's fresh.

▲ *Bilbao cathedral's spire above the streets of Casco Viejo*

# When to go

## SEASONS & CLIMATE

Sitting on Spain's north coast, on the Bay of Biscay, Bilbao has
an Atlantic climate, so you will need to be prepared for rain. The
Atlantic seaboard regions are sometimes called Green Spain, owing
to the amount of rain they receive. Bilbao and these regions are
well known for their wet weather, as celebrated most famously
by the Spanish poet Federico García Lorca in his Galician poems.
Showers should therefore be expected at any time of the year, even
in summer. Luckily, there's a lot to do and see in Bilbao even when
the weather is inclement (see pages 52–3). The area does not get as
hot as it does further south in Spain and there are cooler breezes
to be found, particularly as you climb higher ground. However, the
Basque coast does still get plenty of sun; it is, after all, on the same
latitude as Perpignan in the south of France. You will still need to
take into consideration protection against sunburn and ensure you
cover up exposed skin if you're spending any length of time
outdoors during the summer.

January–February is cool, with maximum temperatures of
9–10°C (48–50°F). Spring weather (March–May) is unsettled, with
marked variations of cold and warmth: the average temperature
can vary between 11°C and 16°C (52–60°F). True summer begins in
June, and until the end of July you can count on warm, dry weather,
averaging 21°C (70°F). August, though still as warm, brings with it
the possibility of thunderstorms, and the rainy season gets going in
September. October is cooler, but still a very pleasant 16°C (60°F),
and this is one of the best months in which to visit; by November
the temperature usually drops sharply as the wet Basque winter
gets under way.

The emergence of no-frills airlines has made Bilbao much more accessible for short breaks from Britain. However, the seasonal fare variations are wide and fares also differ sharply according to the day of the week you choose for your outward and return flights. It pays to investigate thoroughly the offers of different airlines before choosing your dates.

## ANNUAL EVENTS

Bilbao and its surrounding areas host a rich variety of traditional festivals. No matter when you visit you are bound to come across a major or minor celebration.

Fireworks feature in many of the Spanish festivals, and the Basques are happy to oblige with superb displays of their own.

### January
**La Tamborrada, San Sebastián** (20 January) This 24-hour drumming extravaganza sees troupes of uniformed drummers parade through the streets of San Sebastián in high-volume celebration.

### February
**Procession of San Blas** (3 February) San Blas, the Christian martyr famed for feats of miraculous healing, is honoured by a procession through the streets of Bilbao. Stalls selling doughnuts and the coloured cords of San Blas are set up in the Plaza del Arenal. Traditionally, the faithful wear cords around their necks for nine days, having had them blessed in the church of San Nicolás in the plaza, and then burn them; this is said to give protection from throat infections for a year.

**Santa Águeda** (4 February) Choirs in traditional dress take to the streets to sing songs about Santa Águeda, marking time with a staff.

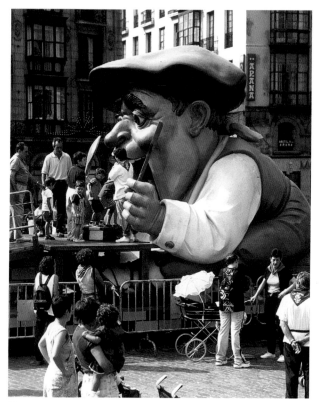

⬤ *Grotesque 'giants', a feature of festivals across the region*

**Carnival** The approach of Lent is the occasion for Carnival, a huge event all over Spain. Bilbao, Vitoria and San Sebastián all have their own carnivals, which involve street processions and cavalcades.

**March–April**
**Easter** Semana Santa, or Easter Week, sees street processions in Bilbao, which begin at the church of Santos Juanes in the Casco Viejo. Revered relics such as the Cristo de la Villa, dating from 1590, are carried around the town. On Easter Sunday the Basques celebrate their national holiday or Aberri Aguna.

**May–June**
**Arrain Azoka** (third weekend in May) This festival is devoted to fish and seafood and takes place in the fishing village of Bermeo.
**Eve of San Juan** (24 June) This pagan bonfire festival is celebrated all over Spain, and in Bilbao is held at Artxanda.
**Summer festivals** From June throughout the summer, there are numerous festivals in small towns and traditional sport shows.

**July**
**Getxo Jazz Festival** This major jazz fest opens the Jazz Festival series in the Basque Country (others are held in Vitoria, San Sebastián and Bayonne). Some concerts are free, but tickets for the

**SMALL TOWN FIESTAS**
These summer fiestas are pagan by tradition but nowadays they are a celebration of the town's saint. During the day there are Basque traditional sports, food competitions, games for children, and at night bonfires and music. Some of the best are Elantxobe, 29 June; Gernika, 15–18 August; Gorliz, 25 July; Lekeitio, 28 June–1 July and 2–6 September; and Bermeo, 7–16 September. For more information, contact the tourist office in Bilbao ☎ 944 795 760

star performances and group competition cost €10–25.
**☎** 944 319 280 **W** www.getxo.net

**International Folklore Festival** Takes place in Portugalete, and attracts folk dancing companies from around the world.

**Jazzaldia** (last week in July) San Sebastián hosts one of the most important jazz festivals in Europe, with outdoor and indoor concerts. **☎** 943 481 900 **W** www.jazzaldia.com **@** infojazz@donostia.org

**Bilboko Kalealdia** This arts festival takes place after the Gexto Jazz Festival and fills Bilbao's streets and squares for six evenings with dance, theatre and circus performances and processions. **W** www.bilbokokalealdia.com

## August

**Aste Nagusia/Semana Grande (Big Week)** On 15 August, for the Feast of the Virgin of Begoña, crowds of the faithful converge on the Basilica de Nuestra Señora de Begoña, east of the old town. From the Saturday following the 15th, citizens celebrate Aste Nagusia, otherwise known as Semana Grande. This is Bilbao's biggest festival, a time for firework displays and street parties, street theatre, and free outdoor pop and rock concerts. During Semana Grande many *bilbaínos*, as locals are known, gather in *konparsas*, cultural and social clubs that organise gastronomy, sports competitions, concerts and theatre at the stands that are set up for the week. Festivals also take place in Vitoria and San Sebastián. **☎** 944 795 760 **W** www.bilbao.net/bilbaoturismo

## September
**San Sebastián International Film Festival** **☎** 943 481 212 **W** www.sansebastianfestival.com

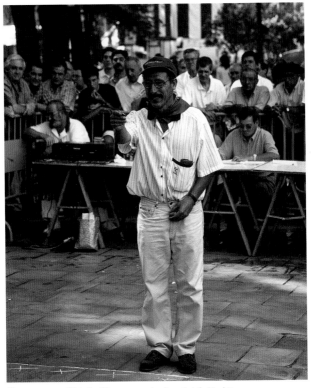

⬤ *You can see all kinds of Basque sports played at festival time*

**Boat Races** (first and second Sunday in September) This major Basque rowing competition, a tradition since 1879, sees 8 teams of 13 compete over a 5-km (3-mile) course. It takes place at the Bahía de la Concha. Ⓦ www.donostiasansebastian.com

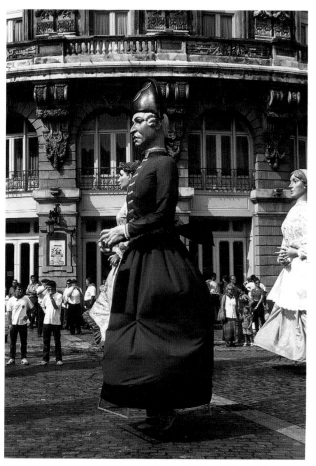

● Parades of 'giants' are a colourful feature of the Aste Nagusia celebrations

**NATIONAL PUBLIC HOLIDAYS**
**New Year's Day** 1 Jan
**Saint Joseph** 19 Mar
**Easter** always March or April
**Labour Day** 1 May
**St James' Day** 25 July
**Assumption** 15 Aug
**Spanish National Day** 12 Oct
**All Saints' Day** 1 Nov
**Constitution Day** 6 Dec
**Immaculate Conception** 8 Dec
**Christmas Day** 25 Dec

**October–December**

**Contemporary Dance and Theatre Festival** Innovative dance and theatre performances take place at La Fundición, Arriaga, Bilborock, Bilbaoescena, CDM San Francisco and Merced Ikastetxea, among other venues. Ⓦ www.badbilbao.com

**International Festival of Documentary and Short Film** Screenings at theatres and cinemas, and also free screenings for up to 30 people in Plaza Arriaga outside the Arriaga Theatre. ⓐ Colón de Larreategui 37 ⓘ 944 248 698 Ⓦ www.zinebi.com

**Festival of Santo Tomás** (21 December) Locals buy fresh produce in time for Christmas at hundreds of stalls selling fresh fruit, vegetables and turkeys, which are set up between Plaza del Arenal and Plaza Nueva in the old town. Shoppers take their refreshment at the many booths selling savoury cooked sausages inside a *talo*, a kind of taco, and glasses of *txakoli* (see page 130).

# Basque Country

Euskal Herria is the name Basque people give to their land, referring to the three provinces that make up the Basque autonomous community: Gipuzkoa, Bizkaia and Alava. There are another four provinces, one on the Spanish side – Navarra, whose capital is Pamplona – and another three on the French side, over the Pyrenees. The Basque language unifies the seven provinces.

The origins of the Basques remain uncertain but the archaeological evidence suggests that they have inhabited the western part of the Pyrenees for thousands of years. Finds date back to as early as the Palaeolithic era, around 9000 BC. Basque people have been described as the last survivors of Europe's original population. Their language, Euskara, stretches back into antiquity and is apparently not related to any other European language. The themes of distinctive Basque pre-Christian myths and legends featuring giants and demons predominate in much of the traditional culture of this region. The Basques absorbed Christianity, at the same time building on their old beliefs to maintain devout religious traditions.

At the outset of the Spanish Civil War in the 1930s, the industrial centres of Bizkaia and Gipuzkoa supported the Republican cause, while the conservative Navarrans and Arabans in neighbouring rural areas joined the Nationalists. An autonomous Basque government was declared in 1936 but the Basques suffered heavily under Franco, starting with the bombing of the city of Gernika by German forces in April 1937. This is often cited as the first civilian target in the history of aerial bombing. Franco's Nationalists made the Basques pay a heavy price for declaring autonomy, killing over 21,000 people. The poet and philosopher Miguel de Unamuno (1864–1937) famously rejected fascism in the face of Nationalist sympathisers and died under house arrest. Although very much a Basque and proud of it, he criticised myth-making about the Basque people and their origins. He spoke out both in support of what he thought was right and to criticise dictators such as Primo de Rivera. It is hard to imagine him tolerating the brutal regime of Franco had he lived on.

With the Nationalist forces' victory, a centralist right-wing administration was imposed on the whole of Spain under Franco's rule; it had little time for regional autonomy and the Basques were repressed. Their language was banned and central government was imposed by force from the outside. Unsurprisingly, this led to a mass exodus of Basques into France and J A Aguirre's Basque government exiled to Paris. There were difficult times for exiled Basques ahead, particularly with the onset of World War II and the rise of the unsympathetic French Vichy regime.

Basque nationalism has always been fiercely asserted throughout its turbulent history. The rise of a more militant version in the shape of ETA (Euskadi ta Askatasuna, 'Basque Homeland and Freedom') earned the region notoriety from the 1960s onwards through a campaign of bombings and assassinations. The restoration of democracy to Spain in the late 1970s/early 80s brought with it a large measure of autonomy for Spain's Basques, including their own parliament and the right to raise taxes. This has fostered a cultural revival, with the Basque language now widely taught and used, and the Basque flag flown publicly throughout the region. Nationalism, in both peaceful and violent forms, is still an influential force, but after the elections of 2009 the Basque Country acquired its first non-Nationalist government of its brief democratic lifetime. This was widely seen as a tentative sign of a new era of pluralist politics and the establishment of a new ceasefire in September 2010 hopefully continues this process.

# History

The Basque people were already well established in this region
when the Romans arrived in the 1st century BC; the Romans prudently
recognised the independence of the tribes of the Vascones, as they
called them, with an agreement on passage and trade, and the
Basques were left pretty much to their own devices. In the early
Middle Ages the Visigoths, Germanic tribes who conquered most of
post-Roman Spain, tried to vanquish the Basque people but they
proved very difficult to overcome, something that numerous
invaders would find over the centuries. The Moors conquered as far
north as Pamplona but never overthrew the people of the Euskal
Herria. The Basques united in 818 to form the Kingdom of Navarra.
They adopted Christianity but kept their own traditions and
customs, such as the *fueros*, the ancient laws under which they
governed themselves.

Bilbao was founded in 1300 by Diego López de Haro, a lord from
Vizcaya. The early city economy was primarily based on fishing and
later on industry. By 1512 the kings of a united Spain gained control
of the Basque region in return for granting it self-government.
This state of autonomy continued for the next two centuries, with
Philip V granting the Basques the right to trade with the newly
discovered Americas. In the same year the Spanish Duke of Alba
divided Navarra in two: south and north, with the latter falling on
the French side.

Napoleon respected their *fueros* in the constitution he drew up
for Spain, in return for their support. Later in the 19th century the
Carlist Wars broke out between the liberals and conservatives.
Most Basques fought alongside the conservatives, as the king,
Charles V, promised he would respect their *fueros*. This acted as a

catalyst for the growth of Basque nationalism in the 19th century and the Basque Nationalist Party was established in 1895.

During the late 19th and early 20th centuries, Bilbao grew to be one of the powerhouses of the Spanish economy on the basis of the surrounding region's mineral deposits. The Banco de Bilbao was founded in 1857 and would later become the embryo of the international BBVA bank. The Altos Hornos de Vizcaya steelworks opened in 1902 and for decades remained the largest company in Spain.

Bilbao's fortunes, however, were shaken by the outbreak of the Spanish Civil War in 1936. The city declared for the Republicans and became a vital objective for Franco, both because of its industry and its symbolic importance to the Basque people. In June 1937, shortly after the bombing of Guernica, the city was besieged by the Nationalists and its loss was a grave blow to Republican hopes of winning the war. Franco exacted revenge against the Basques for opposing him by repressing their language, culture and, above all, ambitions for autonomy.

Bilbao was badly hit by the collapse of traditional industry in the 1980s and 1990s. This did, however, lead to the emergence of a prosperous, modern city, which has dealt positively with its urban sprawl and industrial legacy. The building of the Guggenheim Museum has led the way in the regeneration of this ancient seaport and its new lease of life as a tourist destination, a process now called the 'Guggenheim effect' and much envied by cities around the world in a similar situation. In 2010 the city council became the first winner of the Kuan Yew World City Prize for the 'creation of vibrant, liveable and sustainable urban communities around the world'.

# Lifestyle

The Basque lifestyle is very different from that of the typical North European. Many writers and visitors have commented on the slower pace of life. There is a greater emphasis on social time in cafés and bars and talking to friends, especially on Thursday and Friday nights, and at weekends. The family is held in high esteem as a social institution, and its importance in Basque life would be difficult to overestimate.

Eating is an art in itself in Bilbao, and there are plenty of opportunities to tuck in: cakes and croissants for breakfast, *pintxos* (Basque tapas) to get you through until lunch, three courses for lunch, a small cake in the afternoon or *pintxos* in the evening, and meat, fresh fish and seafood for dinner. In the evening there are late meals that extend far into the night, as the Basques like to take their time eating and relaxing with family and friends.

It is still traditional to take siestas, even if the heat is less intense here than in the south. Many shops and offices close for a couple of hours at lunchtime and don't open until later on in the afternoon. However, this way of life is slowly starting to change, due in part to pressure from the 'North European' model.

The café is at the centre of Bilbao's gregarious, outdoor lifestyle

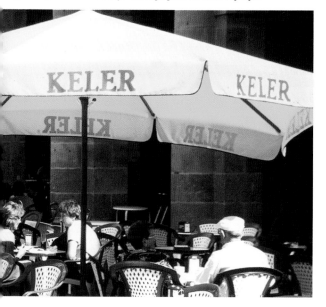

# Culture

So much of culture in Bilbao and its neighbouring areas is bound up in the Basque identity, and the language of the Basques, Euskera, is at the heart of that identity. The first book in Euskera was a collection of poems by Bernart Etxepare in 1545. The decline of the Basque language has been halted in part thanks to the introduction of Basque in schools and the growing awareness among people about the need to use and preserve it.

Basque bards remain popular to this day, and poem improvisers – the traditional Basque version of rappers – are also held in high esteem. Basque music is distinctive, with musicians playing traditional musical instruments (including the *txistu*, a traditional small flute, the wind instrument *alboka*, and the *txalaparta*, on which two people play with wooden sticks) to perform pieces written as far back as the 16th century. Basques love singing and do so with passion. Traditional dances still feature in the villages, especially during fiestas. Some of these can be very lively and even warlike, others more social, in elaborate dress and with fancy steps.

The city of Bilbao has seen a remarkable cultural resurgence. This is reflected in the existence of some splendid museums, galleries and performance centres that are to be found in Bilbao and its neighbouring towns. Cultural highlights include:

**Guggenheim Museum** (see pages 90–91) The Guggenheim almost single-handedly put Bilbao on the cultural tourist map. Although there is much more to the city than this one museum, it remains the must-see attraction, both for its architecture and for the artistic riches it contains.

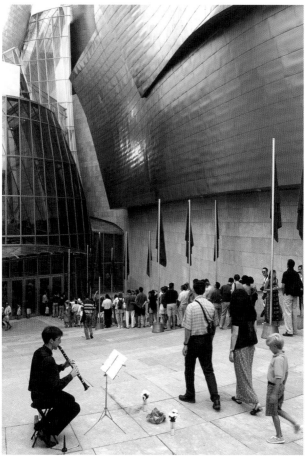

⬥ *The Guggenheim shouldn't be missed, but be prepared for queues at peak times*

**Museo de Bellas Artes (Fine Arts Museum)** (see pages 92–3)
Counterbalancing the modernity of the Guggenheim, this more
traditional art gallery has many treasures by Basque, Spanish and
international artists.

**Museo Marítimo (Maritime Museum)** (see page 94) This new
museum in the old dockyards, commemorating Bilbao's long
association with seafaring, is well worth a visit.

**Museo Vasco** (see pages 71–2) This museum in the old town has
a very mixed collection on the theme of all things Basque, and is
a great way to get an understanding of Basque culture through
the centuries.

**Teatro Arriaga** (see page 72) Not only an architectural jewel inside
and out, this neo-Baroque theatre is a venue for performances of
opera, dance and drama.

**Bridges** The many bridges over the Río Nervión are worth an
itinerary of their own, demonstrating the art of bridge building from
medieval times (those connecting the old town with new Bilbao),
through the 19th century (the engineering tour de force of the
Puente Colgante; see pages 86–8) to graceful modern structures
such as the Puente Zubizuri (see page 84).

▶ *Plaza Nueva*

# MAKING THE MOST OF
Bilbao

# Shopping

## WHERE TO SHOP

Bilbao affords plenty of opportunities for shopping. The two main shopping areas are the Gran Vía, a broad pedestrianised street that runs across the north of modern Bilbao from the Plaza Circular to the Plaza del Sagrado Corazón, and the Casco Viejo (or old town).

Some of Bilbao's finest shops and department stores are located on the Gran Vía, and in the section between Plaza Moyúa and Plaza Circular and around. You will find Basque designer Ion Fiz's shop, local chain stores such as clothing store For (ⓦ www.for.es) and big chains such as Mango, Custo and El Corte Inglés. The latter is a branch of Spain's best-known department store chain, offering a huge range of merchandise, from fashion, books and cosmetics to household and sporting goods.

The Casco Viejo has always been a shopping area and many of its streets, such as Calle Sombrerería (Milliners' Street), still carry the names of the trades in which they specialised. The area still has many independent, traditional shops (particularly shoe shops), as well as new young designers and chain stores. The main shopping streets of the old centre include the Siete Calles (see page 71), Calle Bidebarrieta and Calle Correo.

The most central shopping mall is **Zubiarte** (ⓐ Lehendakari Leizaola 2 ⓘ 944 277 380 ⓦ www.zubiarte.com ⓛ 10.00–22.00 daily ⓜ Metro: Abandoibarra), next to the Puente de Deusto, with more than 70 shops, a supermarket, a cinema and numerous cafés and restaurants.

Be warned that shops in the centre of Bilbao are closed on Sundays, with the exception of some bakeries and newsagents.

◆ Gran Via is lined with boutiques and stores of all kinds

## USEFUL SHOPPING PHRASES

**What time do the shops open/close?**
¿A qué hora abren/cierran las tiendas?
*¿A kay ora abren/theeyerran las teeyendas?*

**How much is this?**
¿Cuánto es?
*¿Cwantoe es?*

**Can I try this on?**
¿Puedo probarme esto?
*¿Pwedo probarmeh esto?*

**My size is ... (shoes)**
Mi número es el ...
*Mee noomero es el ...*

**I'll take this one, thank you**
Me llevo éste
*Meh llievo esteh*

**This is too large/too small/too expensive.**
**Do you have any others?**
Es muy grande/muy pequeño/muy caro. ¿Tienen más?
*Es mooy grandeh/mooy pekenio/mooy karo. ¿Teeyenen mas?*

It's not only the small ones that are closed – even big shopping centres on the edge of town shut all day on Sundays.

## MARKETS

Market day is typically the main weekly event of many towns and villages in the region, and markets take place every day of the week in Bilbao. Mercado de la Ribera is a huge covered market where you can find plenty of fresh fruit and vegetables, and from time to time it also holds cultural events.

## WHAT TO BUY

Gifts and souvenirs can be bought all over the city, including at the shops of the galleries and museums, such as the Guggenheim and the Fine Arts Museum. Basque specialities include wood-carving, weaving and other handicrafts. Fine local food and wines are also good buys. The best areas are the Casco Viejo and around the Guggenheim for handicrafts and souvenirs, and the Mercado de la Ribera for fresh food. Fashion boutiques, ranging from international designer outlets such as MaxMara to small independents, can be found throughout the city, but particularly around the Gran Vía. Leatherwear of all kinds is good value.

⬤ *Pick up a souvenir in the Casco Viejo*

# Eating & drinking

Traditional Basque dishes are famous around the world, and for good reason. Because of the region's proximity to the sea, fish and seafood are an important part of Basque cuisine. The riches of the countryside can also be found in tasty meat dishes, along with local vegetables (locally grown red pepper is a key ingredient). *Marmitako* is a fish stew and *bacalao* dishes are based on cod, cooked in a variety of ways, such as *bacalao al pil-pil* (cooked with garlic) or *a la bizkaina* (cooked with dried red peppers). Fish soup is another good option. Tuna and cod feature regularly, as does *merluza* (hake). Tuna is frequently cooked in spices, garlic, tomatoes and aubergines, and *merluza a la koskera* (hake served in a white wine sauce) is a very popular dish in Bilbao. *Txipirones* is baby squid in its own ink or grilled with onions, and elvers (baby eels) are an exquisite (and very expensive) delicacy eaten around Christmas time.

Meat dishes include grilled or oven-cooked lamb chops, and T-bone beef steak is served almost raw, eaten on its own and accompanied by a good Rioja wine or cider. Chorizo is a spicy sausage that is often combined with other dishes. Flat corn cakes, or *talos*, were traditionally eaten like bread; these days they often feature in winter festivals such as Santo Tomás, and can be either savoury or sweet.

The new Basque cuisine, or *nueva cocina vasca*, uses typical Basque staples to create exciting new dishes. Think wild mushrooms, crêpes with spider crabs or sea bass with green pepper.

There are plenty of local tipples, with grapes and apples forming the basis of what is on offer. Wine is the most famous local beverage. Rioja, made on the edge of the Basque region, is the region's best-known red, made mainly with tempranillo grapes, along with

**PRICE CATEGORIES**

The restaurant price guides used in the book are based on the average price of a two-course dinner for one without drinks.

£ up to €25  ££ €25–50  £££ above €50

Navarra clarets. Local *txakoli* is a light fruity drink, with a touch of acidity. *Sidra* (cider) is a local speciality, especially in the countryside. Anis is popular and is sometimes mixed with other drinks, such as cognac, which is also used to flavour coffee (known as a *carajillo*). *Patxaran* is a very popular liqueur made with anis and sloes, which many families still make at home.

No one should leave Bilbao without having spent at least one evening drifting from bar to bar eating tapas, known here as *pintxos*. The city has a wide range of cafés and *tabernas* (pubs or bars). Though the modern part of Bilbao doesn't lack good places to eat and drink, the Casco Viejo, or old town, east of the river, has the richest pickings; try along Calle Santa Maria, Calle Barrencalle Barrena or the Plaza Nueva for some of the best restaurants and *pintxos*.

For the best value when lunching or dining out, always look for the *menú del día*, which is a complete meal of three courses (and often comes with a bottle of wine) for a single, fixed price, usually stated outside the restaurant. Wherever you choose to eat, you will usually find that *la cuenta* (the bill) does not include service, so a tip is in order if you have been served well.

*A typical street scene in Bilbao's Casco Viejo*

## USEFUL DINING PHRASES

**I would like a table for ... people**
Quisiera una mesa para ... personas
*Keyseeyera oona mesa para ... personas*

**Waiter/waitress!**
¡Camarero/Camarera!
*¡Camareroe/Camarera!*

**May I have the bill, please?**
¿Podría traerme la cuenta por favor?
*¿Pordreea trayerme la cwenta por farbor?*

**Could I have it well cooked/medium/rare please?**
¿Por favor, la carne bien hecha/en su punto/poco hecha?
*¿Por fabor, la kahrrne beeyen kotheeda/al poontoh/roha?*

**I am a vegetarian. Does this dish contain meat?**
Soy vegetariano. ¿Tiene carne este plato?
*Soy begetahreeahnoh. ¿Teeyene carneh esteh plahtoh?*

**Where is the toilet (restroom) please?**
¿Dónde están los servicios, por favor?
*¿Donde estan los serbeetheeos, por fabor?*

**I would like a cup of/two cups of/another coffee/tea**
Quisiera una taza de/dos tazas de/otra taza de café/té
*Keyseeyera oona tatha dey/dos tathas dey/otra tatha dey kafey/tey*

# Entertainment & nightlife

The evening is the time to have fun in Bilbao. The city's nightlife comes in all levels of intensity, from an early evening tapas crawl to a late meal, progressing to a late-night bar or club. Dinner is taken later in the evening. A Bilbao night on the town will nearly always begin with some early bar-hopping, and *pintxos* and drinks, at about 19.30. Typically you should wait until 20.00 at the very earliest to think about dinner; the *pintxos* should sustain you until then. If you want to go dancing afterwards try some of the clubs listed on pages 75–9 and 98–100.

## BARS & CLUBS

Start the night in the Casco Viejo with some relaxed early bar-hopping, known as *txikiteo*. Enjoy *poteo* (small glasses of wine) or *zurito* (a small beer), accompanied by *pintxos*. The liveliest bars can be found in this area, and the busiest bars are on Calle Pelota, Calle Barrenkale, Calle Somera, Calle Santa Maria, Calle Jardines and Calle Perro. For outdoor *poteo*, pull up a chair at one of the outdoor cafés on lovely Plaza Nueva.

The bars along Calle Ledesma, next to Plaza Circular, just across the river in the newer part of town, are popular haunts for an early evening bar crawl. Los Jardines de Albia, particularly Café Iruña, is also a good spot for cafés and bars, some of which have live music. Other good bar-hopping areas include Licenciado Poza (very busy on football match Sundays) and around Plaza Indautxu.

## MUSIC

You'll have little trouble finding live music in Bilbao's bars and clubs, but it may pay to do some research before heading out.

The local papers have listings and the *Bilbao Guide* from the tourist office (see page 151) should be consulted for up-to-date details. The Palacio Euskalduna (beyond the Guggenheim) stages concerts, and there is a bandstand in El Arenal, beside the church of San Nicolás, where you can hear music. During street festivals, especially 'Big Week' in August (see page 12), there are plenty of free performances around town.

## THEATRE

Unless your Spanish or Basque is pretty good, or you are into opera, you may find it difficult to enjoy local performances. The two main venues for performances are:

**Teatro Arriaga** Opera, theatre and comedy shows.
ⓐ Pl. Arriaga 1 ⓣ Information 944 792 036, Tickets 944 310 310
ⓦ www.teatroarriaga.com ⓝ Metro: Casco Viejo; Tram: Arriaga

**Palacio Euskalduna de Congresos y de la Música** The Palacio's programme features musicals and plays, concerts and conferences.
ⓐ C/Abandoibarra 4 ⓣ 944 035 000 ⓦ www.euskalduna.net
ⓝ Metro: San Mamés; Tram: Euskalduna

## CINEMA

**Multicines** (ⓐ C/Eskuza ⓝ Metro: San Mamés) and the
**Renoir** (ⓐ Lehendakari Agirre ⓝ Metro: Deusto) offer films in their original language. See local newspapers for more information.

# Sport & relaxation

## SPECTATOR SPORTS

### Football

*Fútbol* is the most popular sport in Spain and the Basque region is no exception, despite its variety of home-grown sports. Athletic Bilbao is based at the Estadio de San Mamés and home matches take place on Sundays. They are popular with families, which makes for a friendly atmosphere. The club is almost regarded as the Basque national team, especially when playing against Real Madrid. Tickets are generally easy to get hold of – either from the stadium itself or from one of the BBK ATMs around town with full-size keyboards – with the exception of big games, or those against other Basque teams such as Real Sociedad de San Sebastián.

**Athletic Bilbao** Ⓦ www.athletic-club.net Ⓜ Metro: San Mamés; Tram: San Mamés

### Pelota

Traditional Basque handball is reputed to be the fastest ball game in the world. Matches can be seen mainly during the summer months, when the championships are held. In Bilbao the game is played both with bare hands or with a bat at the court (*frontón*) at Calle Esperanza 6 (❶ 944 354 740 Ⓜ Metro: Casco Viejo), or you can watch the professionals at **Club Deportivo Bilbao** ❷ C/Alameda Rekalde Ⓜ Metro: Moyúa

### Bullfighting

Bullfights are a typical element of many festivals in the Basque Country. Ernest Hemingway famously wrote about the sport but these days it's the subject of much opposition, not only internationally but also within Spain, from the Asociación Defensa Derechos Animal

## BULLS AND BULLFIGHTS

Bullfighting is huge in Bilbao and the Basque region, where it is seen as an artistic performance. Bullfights are major events, with teams of *corridas* and *toreros* and then the *matador*. A bullfighting programme lasts about two hours. Bullfights are not easy for visitors to get into; tickets are scarce because of the sport's popularity with locals. Buy tickets at the Plaza de Toros or online at Ⓦ www.plazatorosbilbao.com

Bull running (*encierros*), where spectators become participants and literally run away from charging bulls, takes place most famously in Navarra and in Pamplona at the Festival of Los Sanfermines in July.

As well as at Pamplona, bull running takes place in Tudela (last week of July), Falces (with cows, August), Tafalla (August) and Sanguesa (September).

(Ⓦ www.addaong.org). The best *toreros* can be seen during the Semana Grande (see page 12). The Plaza de Toros de Vista Alegre is south of the city centre; tickets cost between €14 and €147.

**Plaza de Toros de Vista Alegre** ⓐ C/Martin Agüero ⓣ 944 448 698
ⓛ 10.30–13.00, 16.00–18.00 Mon–Fri, closed Sat & Sun Ⓜ Metro: Indautxu

## PARTICIPATION SPORTS

Bilbao has a number of *polideportivos* (public sports centres). Those in the Artxanda, Deusto, Rekalde, San Ignazio and Txurdinaga districts share an online booking system (Ⓦ www.bilbaokirolak.com). The entrance fee is roughly €6, and there are additional charges for courts and pitches. If you intend to go more than once, buy a *bono* of five or ten tickets.

◔ Take a stroll along the Nervión

**Polideportivo de Begoña** The largest and best-equipped sports centre in Bilbao, the Begoña sports centre houses two indoor swimming pools, gyms, and squash and tennis courts. It is also a good place to play pelota, traditional Basque handball. ⓐ Circo Amateur del Club Deportivo 2 (Txurdinaga) ⓘ 09.00–21.00 daily ⓝ Metro: Santutxu

**Club Deportivo Bilbao** This private club is situated in the heart of the city, just a short distance from the Guggenheim. It has pelota courts, saunas, gyms and swimming pools, and is a stylish place to keep in shape. There's also a barber, TV lounge and restaurant. ⓐ C/Alameda Rekalde 28 ⓣ 944 231 108 ⓦ www.club-deportivo.com ⓘ 07.00–23.00 daily ⓝ Metro: Moyúa

## Golf

There's a golf course in Bilbao (**Real Sociedad Golf Neguri** ⓣ 944 910 200) and San Sebastián (**Golf de Basozabal** ⓣ 943 472 736 ⓝ Metro: Neguri).

## Riding

The beautiful landscape around Bilbao makes fine territory for horse riding. Riding centres are listed in tourist information offices and brochures.

## Adventure sports

A wide range of activities, including canoeing and kayaking, diving, nature walks, surfing and bicycle hire, all based around the Urdaibai Biosphere Reserve (see page 135), is offered by UR2000, who can also provide instruction. The main office is in Durango. **UR2000** ⓐ Saibigain 1, Dept. 4 ⓣ 946 814 769 ⓦ www.ur2000.com

# Accommodation

Accommodation in Bilbao and on the Basque coast as a whole tends to fall in a higher price category than the rest of Spain. The Basque government has introduced an *agroturismo* homestay programme, for which farmers offer bed and breakfast. Local tourist offices here are very helpful and have full listings of what is available in the area.

The best places to stay in the city are mostly located in the old town, the Casco Viejo, many of them along the Calle Bidebarrieta, which runs from Plaza Arriaga down to the cathedral, and in the streets around it, including Calle Lotería, Calle Santa María, Jardines and Calle Maria Muñoz.

In the city centre the streets off the Plaza Circular near Calle Buenos Aires and Campo Volantín have numerous *pensiones* and hotels. Half an hour away by subway is the pretty coastal town of Getxo, next to the Puente Colgante, which has top hotels with views over the beaches, as well as cheaper hotels – *hostales* – and *pensiones* in town. Reservations can be made at
ⓔ infoturismo@getxo.net

## HOTELS & GUESTHOUSES
You will find room prices advertised in hotel lobbies. The classification is by an official star system and noted on small blue plaques outside the hotel or guesthouse. Reservations may be made

### PRICE CATEGORIES
Ratings used in this book are based on the average price for a double room per night, including breakfast.
£ up to €50   ££ €50–100   £££ above €100

at ☎ 902 877 298 🌐 www.bilbaoreservas.com. The accommodation categories are as follows:

- *Hotels* Rated from 1 to 5 stars, based on their services.
- *Paradores* Usually state-run historical buildings that have been restored as hotels; can be pricey in high season.
- *Hostales and Pensiones* Typically cheap and cheerful B&Bs, often run by families.
- *Agroturismos* Family-run farmhouses open to the public, usually located in beautiful rural areas.

## HOTELS

**Artetxe Hotel ££** A traditional Basque farmhouse on the hills overlooking Bilbao that's now a warm, family-run hotel with 12 rustic rooms. There's a restaurant serving classic Basque cuisine. ⓐ Carretera Enékuri-Artxanda km 7 ☎ 944 74 77 80 🌐 www.hotelartetxe.com ⓔ info@hotelartetxe.com ⓝ Bizkaibus 3216 to Artxanda

**Barceló Hotel Avenida ££** Large (189-room), mid-range hotel that's geared towards business travellers and conferences, which means that weekend rates are usually moderate. It is near the Basílica de Begoña, just east of the old town. ⓐ Av. Zumalakarregui 40 ☎ 944 124 300 ⓕ 944 114 617 🌐 www.barcelo.com ⓔ avenida@barcelo.com ⓝ Metro: Santutxu

**Husa Jardines de Albia ££** Well-located hotel, just minutes from the Guggenheim, riverside walks, the old town and a metro stop. There's a spa and health club, and the rooms are of a good size and spotlessly clean. The buffet breakfast is excellent. ⓐ C/San Vicente 6 ☎ 944 354 140 🌐 www.hotelhusaspajardinesdealbia.com ⓔ jardinesalbia@husa.es ⓝ Metro/Tram: Abando

**Iturrienea Ostatua ££** One of the nicer choices in the old town, with a blue and yellow façade and plants on balconies. Housed in a lovely Basque town house, decorated in traditional style. ⓐ C/Santa María 14 ⓣ 944 161 500 ⓦ www.iturrieneaostatua.com ⓝ Metro: Casco Viejo

**Ripa ££** A popular hotel with comfortable rooms of a generous size. The location is excellent – on the west bank of the river, overlooking the old town and within walking distance of the Guggenheim and the Gran Vía. Some rooms have balconies with river views. ⓐ C/de Ripa 3 ⓣ 944 239 677 ⓦ www.hotel-ripa.com ⓔ info@hotel-ripa.com ⓝ Metro/Tram: Abando

**Sirimiri ££** Small, peaceful hotel located near the Atxuri tram station.
🅐 Pl. de la Encarnación 3 ☎ 944 330 759 🅦 www.hotelsirimiri.com
🅔 info@hotelsirimiri.com 🅝 Tram: Atxuri

**Vista Alegre ££** A 2-star hotel in the city centre close to the bullring and within walking distance of most of the key sightseeing areas. A hearty breakfast is served in the café. 🅐 C/Pablo Picasso 13 ☎ 944 431 450 🅦 www.hotelvistaalegre.com
🅔 info@hotelvistaalegre.com 🅝 Metro: Moyúa

---

⬇ *Gran Hotel Ercilla's restaurant Bermeo*

**Carlton £££** The best-known hotel in Bilbao, with plenty of history and some famous names in the visitors' book, including Ernest Hemingway. During the Civil War it hosted first the Republican Basque government and then Franco's staff. Located in an elegant building near the Guggenheim. ⓐ Pl. Moyúa ⓣ 944 162 200 ⓦ www.aranzazu-hoteles.com ⓔ carlton@aranzazu-hoteles.com Ⓝ Metro: Moyúa

**Conde Duque £££** Comfortable 3-star Best Western hotel, located on the east bank just north of the Ayuntamiento and a short walk over the bridge from all the sights. The rooms are spacious and well serviced, and there's a restaurant. ⓐ C/Campo Volantín 22 ⓣ 944 456 000 ⓦ www.bestwesternhotelcondeduque.com ⓔ reservas@hotelcondeduque.com Ⓝ Metro: Casco Viejo

**Gran Hotel Ercilla £££** Hotel near Plaza Indautxu that's at the heart of the bullfighting community, especially during the Semana Grande in August. The restaurant, facilities and rooms are top-notch. ⓐ C/Ercilla 37–39 ⓣ 944 705 700 ⓦ www.hotelercilla.es ⓔ ercilla@hotelercilla.es Ⓝ Metro: Indautxu

**Hotel Bilbao Jardines £££** Well situated in the heart of Casco Viejo, the Bilbao Jardines has a classy, modern feel. ⓐ Jardines 9 ⓣ 944 794 210 ⓦ www.hotelbilbaojardines.com ⓔ info@hotelbilbaojardines.com Ⓝ Metro: Casco Viejo; Tram: Arriaga

**Mirohotel £££** Bilbao's first boutique hotel, designed by Antonio Miró, and filled to the rafters with unique design pieces. Cool and comfortable, it's right opposite the Guggenheim and there's even a spa. ⓐ Alameda Mazarredo 77 ⓣ 946 611 880 ⓦ www.mirohotelbilbao.com ⓔ info@mirohotelbilbao.com Ⓝ Metro: Moyúa

**Silken Indautxu £££** A large hotel in the middle of the city, near Plaza Indautxu, that's housed in a handsome white building with a classy glass extension at the back. The interior is slick, and provides all the expected 5-star facilities and luxuries.
ⓐ Pl. Bombero Etxaniz ⓣ 944 211 198 ⓕ 944 221 331
ⓦ www.hoteles-silken.com Ⓜ Metro: Indautxu

## HOSTALES & PENSIONES

**Pensión de la Fuente £** Small, family-run *pension* in the heart of the old town. Some rooms are en-suite, some have shared bathrooms.
ⓐ C/Sombrereria 2 ⓣ 944 169 989 ⓦ www.pensiondelafuente.com
Ⓜ Metro: Casco Viejo; Tram: Ribera

**Hostal La Estrella ££** Very good value for money and set in a delightful building with rooms of a comfortable standard. The location is quieter than other *hostales* of a similar category. Many of the rooms have balconies. ⓐ C/María Muñoz ⓣ 944 164 066 ⓕ 944 167 066
ⓦ www.laestrellaostatu.com Ⓜ Metro: Abando; Tram: Arriaga

**Zabalburu ££** Centrally located hotel with a friendly atmosphere.
ⓐ C/Pedro Martinez Artola 8 ⓣ 944 43 71 00 ⓕ 944 100 073
Ⓜ Metro: Abando

## YOUTH HOSTEL

**Albergue Bilbao Aterpetxea £** A 30-minute bus ride from the centre of town, this hostel has 48 rooms and 8 floors. Facilities include a laundry, safe deposit, Internet access and a restaurant.
ⓐ Carretera Basurtu-Kastrexana 70 ⓣ 944 270 054
ⓦ www.albergue.bilbao.net ⓔ aterpe@albergue.bilbao.net
Ⓝ Bus: 58 from Casco Viejo, 80 from Termibus

# THE BEST OF BILBAO

There is plenty in Bilbao to fill even a long city break, but if you have only a few days to spare then here's our list of sights and experiences you should really try not to miss.

## TOP 10 ATTRACTIONS

- **Bilbao Guggenheim Museum** The city's most celebrated attraction is worth a visit for the architecture alone (see pages 90–91).

- **Casco Viejo** Bilbao's atmospheric old quarter, full of charm by day and full of life by night (see page 66).

- **Poteo** Follow the locals and spend an evening sampling tapas, moving from one lively bar to the next (see page 34).

- **People-watching** It's traditional to chill out while enjoying the free entertainment provided by passing human life in all its variety, over a drink or a coffee, perhaps in one of the cafés on the Plaza Nueva (see page 71).

- **Puente Colgante** Bilbao's 'hanging bridge' is a miracle of 19th-century engineering (see pages 86–8).

- **Festivals** There's always a festival of some kind in Bilbao – whether a traditional religious occasion or a modern celebration of music and theatre (see pages 9–15).

- **Mercado de la Ribera** The largest covered market in Spain stands on the banks of the Río Nervión – search out bargains or superb local produce for a picnic (see page 71).

- **Shopping the Gran Vía** Shop till you drop in the department stores and boutiques of Bilbao's main thoroughfare (see pages 26 and 82).

- **Bilbao Tour** Hop on the red double-decker and admire the city, getting off and on as many times as you want.
  🅐 Lersundi 17, alongside Plaza del Ensanche
  🅦 www.busturistikoa.com

- **Take the train up the mountain** The Artxanda funicular railway takes you out of the city's bustle to the top of Artxanda mountain (see page 82).

🔻 *The Guggenheim Museum has been a key factor in Bilbao's regeneration*

# Suggested itineraries

### HALF-DAY: BILBAO IN A HURRY

If you only have half a day to spend in Bilbao, your time will be best spent wandering around the Casco Viejo, taking in the sights. The ancient centre of the city is small enough to get around in a morning or afternoon and will give you a flavour of this Basque capital. The attractions include the cathedral, the Catedral de Santiago, the Church of Nicolas de Bari and the Teatro Arriaga. Save some time for kicking back in one of the delightful cafés, such as those on the Plaza Nueva.

### 1 DAY: TIME TO SEE A LITTLE MORE

A lot can be done and seen in one day in Bilbao, but you will want to pace yourself. Devote the morning to the Casco Viejo, taking in the atmosphere, and the cathedral and churches. After lunch

● *Walking the picturesque riverside is well worth an hour or two of your time*

(remember that lunch here is usually late and leisurely), cross the
Río Nervión at the Puente del Arenal, so that you don't miss the
view across the river to the Ayuntamiento (town hall) as you stroll
along the Muelle de Urbitarte towards the Guggenheim Museum,
where the architecture and the art on display will easily occupy an
afternoon. You could even forgo lunch in the old quarter and eat
instead at the museum's excellent restaurant. You shouldn't miss
'el Goog' (as the locals call the museum), but if shopping is more your
thing, take a look at the outside and then head down to the Gran Vía
for an afternoon's browsing in the shops and department stores.

## 2–3 DAYS: TIME TO SEE MUCH MORE

This allows you some time to do some justice to the sights of the
city and take in a spot of shopping. Depending on your interests,
you could happily devote a whole day to the Guggenheim Museum,
stopping off in the café and restaurant. Another day can easily be
spent on the other attractions of the city, such as the cathedral
and the Museo de Bellas Artes (see pages 92–3), stopping off in one
of the cafés en route. Explore the Casco Viejo, the covered market,
the Mercado de la Ribera (see page 71) on the edge of the old town,
or the Basque Museum. In the evening head back to the Casco Viejo
for *pintxos* and drinks, followed by a traditional Basque meal in one
of the restaurants in there.

## LONGER: ENJOYING BILBAO TO THE FULL

If you have sampled all of the above and have time to spare, use it to
explore the streets of the Ensanche, the northern part of modern
Bilbao near the river. One or more days should be set aside for an
expedition or two outside Bilbao: both San Sebastián and Vitoria
justify a day or two as well.

# Something for nothing

Much of what Bilbao has to offer costs nothing to enjoy. If you like museums, remember that many of them are free on Wednesdays or Thursdays (not the Guggenheim, unfortunately), and that galleries are free every day. However, many other attractions are free of charge all the time – in particular, churches such as the Catedral de Santiago, the Church of San Nicolás, the shrine of the Vizcayans and the Basílica de Begoña (great for views of the old quarter).

Of course, there is no charge for walking the streets and soaking up the plentiful vistas and atmospheric street life. You can easily while away the hours wandering the streets of the Casco Viejo or Siete Calles, the seven original streets of old Bilbao, the historical heart of the city. The old run-down quarter, near Calle San Francisco

● *The Mercado de la Ribera, moored in the old town*

on the other side of the river, is being revitalised by a variety of new alternative shops selling books, furniture and clothes, and a choice of restaurants; check out Calle Dos de Mayo in particular.

Watching people come and go in the squares such as Plaza Nueva, with its neoclassical arches, is a time-honoured Bilbao pastime. Sunday afternoon and evening is the time to see local families out and about. Another great place for people-watching is the daily covered market, the Mercado de la Ribera. If you want somewhere cultural to hang out for a while, try the Alhóndiga arts and leisure centre (⒜ Pl. de Arriquibar 4 ⓘ 944 014 014 ⓦ www.alhondigabilbao.com ⓛ 07.00–23.00 daily ⓜ Metro: Indautxu), a 1909 wine store recently rehabilitated in an ultra-modern style by Philippe Starck. Some of its facilities and events cost money, but you can wander around the building and browse in the shop for free.

# When it rains

Unless you visit Bilbao in the height of summer (see page 8) you are likely to experience a rainy day, or half-day, but it doesn't have to be a washout as the city has many undercover attractions.

The Bilbao Guggenheim Museum, with its magnificent titanium architecture that seems to glow even on dull days, is your first stop when it rains. It could keep you occupied for a whole day of inclement weather, and you don't even have to go outside in search of refreshment, as the museum has a good café and restaurant.

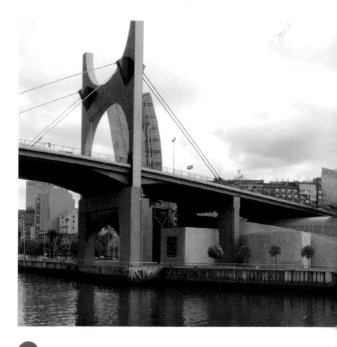

However, Bilbao's museums don't end with the Guggenheim – visit the Museo de Bellas Artes at Parque de Doña Casilda Iturrizar, the Museo Vasco in the old town, the Museo de Arte Sacro or the rather eccentric Museo de Reproducciones Artísticas (ⓦ www.museoreproduccionesbilbao.org). If you find yourself in the Casco Viejo when the clouds burst, hurry along to the Plaza Nueva or to a pórtico of Calle Ribera. The Mercado de la Ribera, the covered market by the river, is a fine spot to sample some interesting local produce under cover.

🔽 *Cross the Puente de La Salve to the Guggenheim*

# On arrival

### TIME DIFFERENCE
Spain follows Central European Time (CET). During Daylight Saving Time (late Mar–late Sept) the clocks are put ahead one hour.

### ARRIVING
#### By air
Bilbao's modern airport at Loiu, designed by Santiago Calatrava, is worth visiting for its architecture alone. Northern Spain's busiest airport, it is located 12 km (7 miles) north of the city. Facilities include four cafeterias, shops and a bureau de change. For car hire at the airport, see pages 63–4.

The yellow Bizkaibus A-3247 runs every 30 minutes from 06.20 until 24.00 from just outside the Arrivals section, taking about 20 minutes to go into town, where it stops at Alameda Recalde, Plaza Moyúa and the Gran Vía before reaching the Termibús bus station; the fare is €1.30. Taxis are also available from outside Arrivals – expect to pay around €20 to the city centre.
**Bilbao Airport** Ⓦ www.aena.es

#### By rail
Rail-based visitors coming from the UK via San Sebastián (see page 140) arrive at the Estación de Atxuri, which serves the Euskotren regional railway. This is located just south of the old town on the east bank of the river. To reach the city centre more quickly, alight at the suburban station of Bolueta, where there is an interchange with the metro to the city centre. Those arriving from other parts of Spain on RENFE (Spanish state railways) trains will arrive at the Estación de Abando on the Plaza Circular, in the heart of the city.

### By road

Long-distance buses arrive at the large Termibús bus station
(ⓐ C/Guturbay 1 ① 944 395 077) one block away from the San Mamés
station on the western edge of the centre. The nearest metro station
is San Mamés; there are also tram and local train connections.

Most drivers will arrive from the direction of France on the A8
*autopista* (motorway). There are three well-signposted exits from
the motorway into the heart of Bilbao.

### By water

The ferry terminal is north of the city at Santurtzi and is connected
by bus and train services to the city centre. ⓐ Av. Cristóbal Murrieta,
Santurtzi ① 944 839 494 ⓝ Bizkaibus A-3151, non-stop to Plaza Jado;
RENFE: train from Santurtzi station to Estación Abando

### FINDING YOUR FEET

It is easy to acclimatise to Bilbao. It's not a large city and the pace
is manageable, plus the streets are laid out on a fairly regular
rectangular grid (apart from in the old town), making it difficult
to get lost.

Bilbao is generally safe for tourists, with lower levels of crime
than the UK. ETA, at time of writing, have a new ceasefire in
place; travellers should consult the Foreign Office travel advice
(ⓦ www.fco.gov.uk) for the latest on the risk of terrorism. It should
also be noted that traffic accident figures are higher than in the UK.
Caution is needed when driving and also when crossing roads on
foot; this especially applies to UK and other tourists used to traffic
approaching from the right.

Levels of petty crime are lower than in the tourist areas down
south. The usual sensible precautions are advised when walking

about the city, especially at night or alone. The red-light district (or *barrio chino*, as it is known locally) near the Calle San Francisco, south of the railway station, is not for the faint-hearted at night – during the day, however, it is usually all right for wandering around, with a variety of restaurants.

## ORIENTATION

The centre of modern Bilbao is bounded by the River Nervión to the north and east. It consists of a number of grand squares or plazas

### IF YOU GET LOST, TRY...

**Excuse me, do you speak English?**
Perdone, ¿habla usted inglés?
*Pairdohneh, ¿ahbla oosteth eengless?*

**Excuse me, is this the right way to the old town/the city centre/the tourist office/the station/the bus station?**
Perdone, ¿por aquí se va al casco antiguo/al centro de la ciudad a la oficina de turísmo/a la estación de trenes/a la estación de autobuses?
*Pairdohneh, ¿por akee seh bah ah el kasko antigwo/al thentroe de la theeoodath/offeetheena deh toorismoe/la estatheeon de trenes/estatheeon dey awtoebooses?*

**Can you point to it on my map?**
¿Puede señalármelo en el mapa?
*¿Pwede senyarlarmeloe en el mapa?*

linked by roads and avenues. The old centre, the Casco Viejo, is a distinctive quarter located on the east bank of the river. The Siete Calles, the seven original medieval streets of old Bilbao, are on the south side of the old quarter, encircled by Calle La Ronda. The Plaza Nueva remains the heart of the old city, where you will find cafés, bars and shops. In the middle of the old quarter stands the cathedral, the Catedral de Santiago, which is a distinctive feature on the Bilbao skyline and a useful landmark. The Mercado de la Ribera, the big covered market, is found on the east bank at the south of the old quarter. At the northern end of the old quarter is the district of El Arenal; here you'll find the San Nicolás de Bari Church and, opposite, the Teatro Arriaga and a tourist office (see page 150). Further up the east bank is the imposing town hall, and, opposite, Basque sculptor Oteiza's magnificent work *The Ovoid Variation of the De-occupation of the Sphere*.

The banks of the Nervión are linked by several bridges, chief of which are the Puente del Arenal and Puente del Ayuntamiento. On the west bank is the modern city centre, called the Ensanche (Extension), developed to allow expansion across the river and now the commercial and business centre of Bilbao. The Puente del Arenal leads westwards to the Plaza Circular, whose distinctive feature is the tall grey building of the Banco Bilbao Vizcaya Argentaria (BBVA), dating from the 1960s. From the Plaza Circular, the Gran Vía is Bilbao's premier shopping street, running across the Ensanche all the way to the Plaza del Sagrado Corazón, where it meets up with the river again at the Puente Euskalduna, overlooked by the large Palacio Euskalduna conference and event centre. Just south of it is the home of Athletic de Bilbao, the San Mamés Stadium.

The westward loop of the river forms the northern boundary of the modern centre and at the northernmost point stands the

Guggenheim Museum; on the north bank is the centenary University of Deusto. Down the river, the 19th-century Puente Colgante links Portugalete and Getxo. The bridge was named a UNESCO World Heritage Site in 2006.

## GETTING AROUND

Central Bilbao can be explored on foot without difficulty, since nearly all the attractions are within walking distance of each other. Nevertheless, if you need to cover the city quickly, there's a well-developed public transport system.

The modern, award-winning metro (subway) system has stations designed by Norman Foster; entrances to them are distinctive steel-and-glass tubular structures known to the locals as *fosteritos*. The two lines run from the northern outskirts to Etxebarria in the south, crossing the centre of town with four useful central stops (west to east): San Mamés (by the football stadium but also useful for the bus station), Moyúa (halfway along the Gran Vía), Abando (at the main railway station and next to the Puente del Arenal) and Casco Viejo (on the eastern edge of the old town). Line 2 connects with the ferry terminal at Santurtzi (see page 55). Within the city centre journeys are a flat fare (€1.40). ⓦ www.metrobilbao.net

Complementing the metro is the even newer tram line. This usefully stops at some of Bilbao's landmarks, such as the Teatro Arriaga, the Guggenheim Museum, the Euskalduna Palace and the San Mamés stadium. You must validate your ticket before getting on. There are also red city buses run by Bilbobus (ⓦ www.bilbao.net), whose routes are displayed at *paradas* (bus stops). Flat-fare single tickets for trams and buses are €1.20, but you get a much better rate by using a *Creditrans* pass or by buying a multi-journey ticket (see box page 64).

## CAR HIRE

Driving Bilbao's traffic-packed streets is not recommended, but you may want to hire a car to visit some of the out-of-town destinations, stopping and making the most of the beautiful scenery and village life. Very often the best-value rates are obtainable by booking in advance through your airline or travel agent or on the Internet, but if you haven't done so and want to hire a car at the airport, try any of the following:

**Avis** ❶ 944 869 649 ❶ 944 531 209 Ⓦ www.avis.es
🕒 07.00–23.30 daily
**Europcar** ❶ 944 869 780 ❶ 944 710 000 Ⓦ www.europcar.es
🕒 07.30–23.30 Mon–Fri, 08.00–23.00 Sat & Sun
**Hertz** ❶ 944 530 931 ❶ 944 530 552 Ⓦ www.hertz.es 🕒 07.00–24.00
Mon–Fri, 07.30–23.30 Sat & Sun

⬤ *Bilbao's distinctive metro entrances are easy to spot*

## TRANSPORT BARGAINS

Sold in denominations of €5, €10 and €15, **Creditrans** is a multi-journey travel ticket that can be used on the metro, buses and trams (and probably trains in the future). Alternatively, buy a **BilbaoCard** from one of the tourist offices, which gives low fares on local transport and museums, and discounts at some shops and restaurants, leisure facilities and shows (one day €6, two €10 and three €12).

**National Atesa** ① 944 533 340 ① 944 530 359 ⓦ www.atesa.es
🕐 07.00–23.30 Mon–Fri, 07.00–23.00 Sat & Sun

The local Yellow Pages lists many local car hire firms in the city centre.

❍ *Puente Zubizuri links the banks of the Río Nervión*

# THE CITY OF
## Bilbao

# Old Bilbao

The Casco Viejo is the old centre of the city. The oldest monuments and sights are in this quarter, also known as Siete Calles after the seven founding streets. Its pedestrianised streets are full of Basque flavour with plenty of shops, bars and restaurants, as well as the cathedral, churches, the Basque Museum, and the nearby Teatro Arriaga and Paseo del Arenal.

## SIGHTS & ATTRACTIONS

There are numerous sights and attractions in the Casco Viejo. The best way to take them in is by simply wandering around the maze of lanes, soaking up the atmosphere. In addition to the sights below, there are plenty of bars, cafés and restaurants, in particular on or near the Plaza Nueva.

### Biblioteca Municipal de Bidebarrieta (Bidebarrieta City Library)

This wonderful building, erected between 1888 and 1890 by Severino de Achúcarro in an eclectic style, is one of the old town's finest structures. It used to be home to the Sociedad El Sitio, a society established in 1975 by liberals. Floods in 1983 caused serious damage but it was subsequently fully refurbished. A working library, it has a computer room on the ground floor with free Internet access.

ⓐ C/Bidebarrieta 4 ⏰ 08.30–20.30 Mon–Fri, 10.30–14.00 Sat (summer); closed Mon morning (winter) Ⓜ Metro: Casco Viejo; Tram: Arriaga

### Bolsa de Bilbao (Old Exchange Building)

Built in 1725 to house the stock exchange, the Baroque Edificio de la Bolsa is today a civic centre. In the building opposite you'll find

a small figure of the Virgin Begoña. If you stand by the figure you can see the Basílica de Begoña – the only place in the Siete Calles where this is possible, due to the old town's narrow streets.
@ C/Pelota 10 @ Metro: Casco Viejo; Tram: Arriaga

### Catedral de Santiago (Cathedral of St James)

The first church on this site was built in the 13th century. It was expanded from the 14th to the 16th centuries, which is when the Gothic style was implemented, along with the portico, cloister, sacristy and the beautiful Puerta del Angel doorway, which contains a pilgrim's shell, the symbol of the pilgrims' route to Santiago de Compostela. It became a cathedral in the 1950s and remains a stopping point for pilgrims. @ Pl. Santiago 1 @ 944 153 627 @ Daily
@ Metro: Casco Viejo; Tram: Ribera

### Church of San Nicolás de Bari

Standing at the centre of the small El Arenal quarter, this is a church worth exploring. It dates from the middle of the 18th century and was constructed on the ruins of an earlier chapel. The octagonal Baroque interior contains sculptures by the Basque artist Juan de Mena. Opposite the church stands the Bilbao Bank Building, the first office of the Banco de Bilbao when it was founded in 1857. Today it houses a cultural exhibition centre and historical archive. Nearby is the Paseo del Arenal, where a flower market is held on Sundays.
@ C/Esperanza 1 @ Daily except during Mass @ Metro: Casco Viejo

### Fuente del Perro (Dog Fountain)

This fountain, one of Bilbao's most popular sights, is a small and unusual neoclassical monument remodelled in 1800 from a previous fountain. Despite the name, it was constructed to provide drinking

○ *The late 19th-century Teatro Arriaga is one of Bilbao's key cultural centres*

water for humans, not dogs. People started to call it 'del Perro' after the three vaguely canine-looking figures that form the spouts (they are meant to be lions' heads). The Calle del Perro is also a good place to find watering holes of a different kind – it's one of the old town's best areas for bars. ❸ C/del Perro Ⓜ Metro: Casco Viejo; Tram: Arriaga

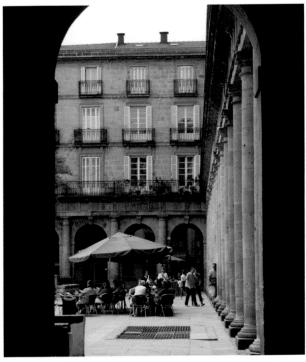

⬤ Take a well-earned break in neoclassical Plaza Nueva

### Mercado de la Ribera

A short distance from San Antón along the Calle de la Ribera, and located on the banks of the Río Nervión, is the largest covered market in the country. It sells local produce and is Bilbao's premier fish market, which is a big deal in a city that prides itself on seafood. The market building dates from 1929. After the flooding in 1983 it was refurbished and its interior modernised. From time to time the market holds cultural events, from theatre to exhibitions. 🕐 08.00–14.00, 16.30–19.00 Mon–Fri, 08.30–14.30 Sat, closed Sun Ⓜ Metro: Casco Viejo; Tram: Arriaga

### Plaza Nueva

There are 64 arches around this enclosed square, built in 1821 in a neoclassical style. It's the perfect spot to take a break, with plenty of cafés and bars; it also has an outdoor flea market on Sunday mornings. Euskaltzaindia, the Basque Language Academy's head office, is on the plaza. Ⓜ Metro: Casco Viejo

### Siete Calles (Seven Streets)

The very oldest part of Bilbao shows the shape of the medieval city, and is bounded by the 'round street', Calle de la Ronda, whose shape follows the line of the old city walls. At the southern end is the 15th-century church of San Anton, dedicated to the patron saint of farmers. Ⓜ Metro: Casco Viejo

## CULTURE

### Museo Arqueológico, Etnográfico e Histórico Vasco
### (Museum of Basque Archaeology, Anthropology and History)

The Museo Vasco (Euskal Museoa in Basque), housed in a building that was once part of a Jesuit church dating from the early 17th

century, is an interesting exploration of Basque life, from prehistorical
times up to the 20th century. It explores traditional ways of living,
beliefs and occupations, both inland and in the fishing villages
along the coast. In the delightful cloister there is a Mikeldi stone
sculpture dating from the Iron Age. ❸ Pl. Miguel Unamuno 4
❶ 944 155 423 Ⓦ www.euskal-museoa.org Ⓛ 11.00–17.00 Tues–Sat,
11.00–14.00 Sun, closed Mon Ⓜ Metro: Casco Viejo ❶ Admission
charge (free Thur)

### Teatro Arriaga

The Teatro Arriaga is the most beautiful building in El Arenal, with
a neo-Baroque frontage. It is named after the 'Spanish Mozart', the
Bilbao-born child prodigy Crisóstomo de Arriaga. Built by Joaquín
Rucoba and Octavio de Toledo, it was opened in 1890 and is often
said to resemble the Garnier Opéra in Paris. The façade has large
balconies supported by Atlantean figures. In 1914 it was burned
down and has since gone through a number of changes. The
magnificent interior, refurbished in 1986, contains antique furniture
and carpets made by the Real Fábrica Nacional de Tapices
(Royal National Tapestry Manufacturers). Today the building
functions as the city's main theatre, with a full programme of
drama, opera, ballet, music and other cultural events.
❸ Pl. Arriaga ❶ Information 944 792 036, Tickets 944 310 310
Ⓦ www.teatroarriaga.com Ⓜ Metro: Casco Viejo; Tram: Arriaga

### RETAIL THERAPY

This is the oldest shopping area in the city. It has a large
number of independent boutiques, as well as many chain stores,
offering something for just about all tastes and budgets. The main

shopping streets in the Casco Viejo are Calles Ascao, Artekale, Bidebarrieta, Correo, Cruz and Somera.

**Gili-gili** Basque for 'tickling', selling unusual clothing and accessories for women. Ⓐ Lotería 4 Ⓣ 944 790 406 Ⓛ 10.00–14.00, 16.00–20.00 Mon–Sat, closed Sun Ⓝ Metro: Casco Viejo

**La Iguana** The owner chooses items for the home that he loves and mixes them up in this cosy shop. Ⓐ Belostikale 4 Ⓣ 944 155 146 Ⓦ www.laiguanabilbao.com Ⓛ 10.00–13.30, 17.00–20.30 Mon–Sat, closed Sun Ⓝ Metro: Casco Viejo; Tram: Ribera

**Lu-la** A colourful place where you'll find anything from women's clothes, shoes and accessories to items for the home. Ⓐ Cinturería Ⓣ 944 164 372 Ⓦ www.lulabilbao.com Ⓛ 10.00–14.00, 16.00–20.00 Mon–Sat, closed Sun Ⓝ Metro: Casco Viejo

**La Matilda etxeko pitxiak** Home decoration and accessories. Ⓐ Jardines 2 Ⓣ 944 152 089 Ⓦ www.lamatilda.es Ⓛ 10.30–14.00, 17.00–20.30 daily Ⓝ Metro: Casco Viejo; Tram: Arriaga

**Skunk Funk** Fresh-faced Basque fashion. Ⓐ Pl. Nueva 2 Ⓣ 944 152 859 Ⓦ www.skunkfunk.com Ⓝ Metro: Casco Viejo

**Sombrerería Gorostiaga** Founded in 1857 and still selling typical Basque berets (*txapelas*) made on site, as well as a selection of other headwear for men and women. Ⓐ Victor 9 Ⓣ 944 161 276 Ⓛ 10.00–13.30, 16.00–20.00 Mon–Fri, 10.00–13.30 Sat, closed Sun Ⓝ Metro: Casco Viejo; Tram: Arriaga

**Urbana** T-shirts with attitude – clothing for men and women by up-and-coming young designers. ❷ Portal de Zamudio 1 ❶ 944 153 628 🕐 10.00–20.30 daily 🇲 Metro: Casco Viejo

## TAKING A BREAK

There are numerous cafés and *tabernas* in the Casco Viejo, particularly along Calle Santa Maria and Calle Barrenkale Barrena, and on Plaza Nueva. Many of the bars in the After Dark section below open all day and well into the night.

**La Exquisita** £ ❶ This traditional café and cake shop offers typical local sweet treats such as Carolina, a meringue cake named after

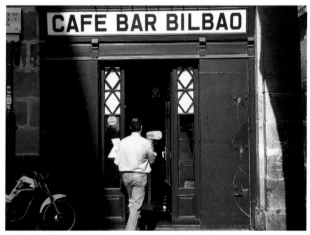

⬤ The old town's best bars are often tucked away in alleys and hidden corners

the confectioner's daughter. ⓐ C/Tendería 4 ① 944 159 085
① 08.30–13.30, 16.00–20.30 Mon–Fri, 08.30–14.00, 16.30–20.30 Sat,
09.00–14.00 Sun ⓝ Metro: Casco Viejo; Tram: Ribera

## AFTER DARK

Bilbao's Casco Viejo is undoubtedly the choice place to head for
*pintxos* and evening drinking, the best areas being on and around
the Plaza Nueva.

### RESTAURANTS & TAPAS BARS

**Zugan £** ❷ Tiny bar that has a huge range of delicious *pintxos*,
and a great terrace with parasols on Plaza Nueva. ⓐ Pl. Nueva 2
① 944 150 321 ① 09.30–22.30 Mon–Fri, 10.00–23.00 Sat, 10.00–16.00 Sun
ⓝ Metro: Casco Viejo

**Asador Arriaga ££** ❸ This *asador* (restaurant specialising in roast
meats) is in the style of a Basque cider house (*sidreria*) and evokes
the countryside. It serves grilled meat and fish cooked in a variety
of local ways and home-made deserts. Customers can help
themselves to the cider directly from the barrels. ⓐ C/Santa María 13
① 944 165 670 ⓦ www.asadorarriaga.com ① 13.00–16.00,
20.30–24.00 daily ⓝ Metro: Casco Viejo

**La Deliciosa ££** ❹ An excellent place to sample Basque cuisine in
the Old Town. It's decorated in the style of a Parisian restaurant
and serves a great selection of dishes, especially seafood such as
the classic cod dish Bacalao a la Vizcaina. ⓐ C/Jardines 1 ① 944 150
944 ⓦ www.ladeliciosa.net ① 13.30–16.00, 20.30–23.30 daily
ⓝ Metro: Casco Viejo

**Victor Montes ££**  This bar and restaurant with lovely *Modernista* décor and a terrace on Plaza Nueva serves Spanish cuisine; *merluza* (hake) and beef dishes are a speciality. Booking advisable.
ⓐ Pl. Nueva 8 ⓣ 944 157 067 ⓦ www.victormontesbilbao.com
ⓛ 10.30–23.00 Mon–Sat, closed Sun Ⓜ Metro: Casco Viejo

**El Perro Chico £££** ❻ Imaginative Basque cuisine over the river from the Siete Calles, next to Puente de la Ribera. It's said that Gehry came across his keynote 'Bilbao blue' in this restaurant.

⬇ *Victor Montes serves up great* pintxos *in the heart of the old town*

C/Aretxaga 2  944 150 519  13.00–17.00, 21.15–01.30 Tues–Sat, closed Mon & Sun  Metro: Casco Viejo; Tram: Ribera

**Mandoya £££ ❼** Succulent Basque cuisine is served in this venerable restaurant, which has been in business for more than 50 years. Meat and fish are cooked *a la brasa* (grilled) to enhance the flavours. There's a good-value, fixed-price menu at lunch time, but if you want to splash out, try the lobster. C/Perro 3–5  944 157 984  www.restaurantemandoya.com  13.30–15.30, 21.00–23.00 daily  Metro: Casco Viejo

## BARS & CLUBS

**Badulake** This bar is one of the best in town, on account of its dance floor, music (from the 70s onwards) and easy-going atmosphere. It's a mixed gay/straight venue. C/Hernani 10 www.badulake.net Metro/Tram: Abando

**Café Bar Bilbao** Good coffee and *pintxos*, and a nice terrace with friendly staff. Pl. Nueva 6 944 151 671 07.00–24.00 daily, closed Sun evening Metro: Casco Viejo

You can't leave Bilbao without sampling the **pintxos**

**K2** A pub popular for its huge range of tasty sandwiches and photography exhibitions. There's dancing from midnight onwards. ⓐ C/Somera 10 ⓣ 944 163 450 ⓛ 10.00–02.00 Mon–Thur, 10.00–03.00 Fri, 12.00–03.00 Sat & Sun Ⓜ Metro: Casco Viejo; Tram: Ribera

**Lamiak** Studenty café-bar with good music. ⓐ C/Barrenkalle Barrena 7 ⓣ 944 159 642 ⓛ 15.30–01.30 Mon–Fri, 16.00–02.00 Sat & Sun Ⓜ Metro: Casco Viejo; Tram: Ribera

# Modern Bilbao

On the left bank, west and south of the Río Nervión, is the larger part of the city centre, stretching west and north from the Plaza Circular on the west side of the Puente del Arenal (for map see pages 56–7). Most places of interest for tourists are located in the northern districts of this area, which are collectively known as the Ensanche, or Extension, so named when, in the 19th century, the city's prosperity and industrialisation caused it to spread outside the old city. At its northernmost point, by the river, the old shipyard and docks area has been revitalised by the opening of the famous Bilbao Guggenheim Museum (see pages 90–91); further north, over the Puente de Deusto, is the Deusto district, site of the University of Deusto.

## SIGHTS & ATTRACTIONS

### Deusto

To get to the suburb of Deusto, either cross the Puente de Euskalduna (leading off Plaza del Sagrado Corazón) or the older Puente de Deusto, which can be reached from Plaza de Federico Moyúa via Calle Elcano. Stroll along the Ribera de Deusto for good views, especially of the Palacio Euskalduna, the Guggenheim and Isozaki Atea. Located in this suburb is the grand-looking Universidad de Deusto, established in the 19th century by Jesuits. It is a prestigious place of learning, particularly in the field of business studies and law. The university has shown commitment to the Basque language, and created the first degree in Basque philology. It is located opposite the Guggenheim, and linked by a pedestrian bridge. The Deusto district caters to its student population with plenty of bars, cafés and restaurants. The district used to be a town, and retains a separate identity.

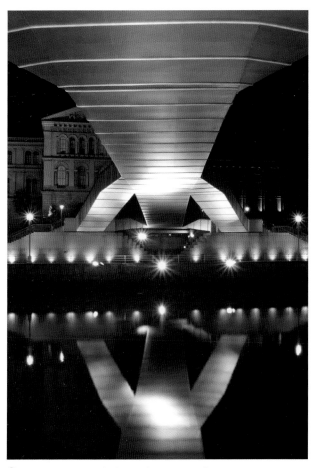

◆ *The Puente de Deusto, leading to the University of Deusto*

## Funicular de Artxanda

For a breath of fresh air, take this delightful funicular railway on the 800-m (¹/₂-mile) trip to the top of the Artxanda mountain (leaves every 15 minutes), from where you'll get panoramic views of the whole city and the river estuary. There are many restaurants and bars in the area, where you can taste *txakolis*, young white wines from the region.

ⓐ C/Castaños ⓛ 07.15–22.00 Mon–Fri, 08.15–22.00 Sat & Sun
Ⓝ Metro: Casco Viejo

## Gran Vía De Don Diego López de Haro

Modern Bilbao's main thoroughfare, named after the city's founding father, begins at the Plaza Circular and continues across the city centre as far as the Plaza del Sagrado Corazón. This is the shopping and business centre of Bilbao. Halfway along the Gran Vía you'll come to Plaza de Federico Moyúa, a large roundabout with flower gardens at its centre and an attractive geometric layout. On it are two large buildings: the colourful Palacio de Chávarri, dating back to 1894 and seat of the Spanish local government, and the 5-star Carlton Hotel, which was the Basque government's headquarters during the Civil War. The Carlton, built in 1927, is on the city's cultural heritage list and is well worth a look inside. As you continue west along the Gran Vía, you'll be walking parallel to the Parque de Doña Casilda de Iturrizar, the site of the Museo de Bellas Artes (see pages 92–3), and you'll eventually come to the Plaza del Sagrado Corazón.

### The Nervión's bridges

The bridges over the Río Nervión, old and new, are key features of Bilbao's cityscape, offering interesting views. Most of them

◆ *Plaza de Federico Moyúa bisects the Gran Vía*

are architecturally significant, and connect with riverside walks, enabling you to cross and re-cross the river.

Heading upstream from the Puente Colgante (Hanging Bridge; see pages 86–8), you come to the 1990s Puente Euskalduna, which curves high across the river and has a striking covered pedestrian walkway. The old Puente de Deusto is a bascule bridge, once essential for letting ships pass, and is reminiscent of London's Tower Bridge. Next is the pedestrian wooden bridge that links the Guggenheim and the University of Deusto.

Puente de la Salve was a 1970s addition to Bilbao's riverscape. The original bridge was where Basque sailors could get a glimpse of the Begoña Basilica from the estuary, chanting a prayer to the Virgin Mary, a pious custom recalled in a small monument. Today you can take a lift up here, which gives you one of the city's best views of the Guggenheim Museum.

The Puente Zubizuri, or White Bridge, is a graceful suspension bridge designed by Santiago Calatrava, architect of the new Bilbao Airport, and is named after the white concrete and white steel from which it is built. It spans the Nervión between the Guggenheim and the Ayuntamiento, connecting Campo Volantín with Mazarredo over the Izosaki Atea. You can cross it to get the funicular railway up to Artxanda (see page 82).

Further upriver, the Puente de Ayuntamiento, or town hall bridge, used to be a drawbridge like the Deusto, but the mechanism hasn't been used for many years.

### Palacio Euskalduna de Congresos y de la Música (Euskalduna Palace)

This large, state-of-the-art conference and performance venue was built as part of the regeneration of Bilbao in the 90s. The shape of the building, designed by Federico Soriano and Dolores Palacios, represents the last ship built in the old Euskalduna shipyard on this site. Its auditorium can hold up to 2,200 spectators and has an extraordinary symphonic organ. The nearby curved Euskalduna Bridge was inaugurated in 1997. ❷ Av. Abandoibarra 4 ❶ 944 035 000 Ⓦ www.euskalduna.net ❸ info@euskalduna.net Ⓝ Metro: San Mamés; Tram: Euskalduna

**Paseo de Uribitarte**

The esplanade starts opposite El Arenal and runs along the river all the way to Avenida de Abandoibarra and beyond, through an area that was once the industrial centre of the city (though few buildings from that period remain). As you walk along it, you'll see the new Isozaki Atea, the Zubizuri Bridge, Euskalduna and the Guggenheim; you'll also get views of the town hall to the east side

⬥ *Calatrava's Puente Zubizuri makes an elegant approach to the city centre*

of the river. Isozaki Atea (*isozaki* means door in Basque) is a development designed by the Japanese architect Arata Isozaki, which comprises two skyscrapers and 1,000 sq m (10,764 sq ft) between the two buildings, where wide stairs connect the lower part of the riverside with the upper town. Halfway up take a look at Eduardo Chillida's sculpture *Looking for the Light*. Parque de Doña Casilda is nearby, and along Paseo de Uribitarte you'll come across green areas and children's playgrounds. On the other side of the river there is an older, tree-lined esplanade called Paseo Campo de Volantín.

## Puente Colgante

Bizkaia's most unusual bridge is up there with Bilbao's biggest attractions. The task faced by the city fathers in the 1880s was to build a bridge near the mouth of the estuary, which would not obstruct the passage of the large ocean-going vessels on which Bilbao's commerce, heavy industry and shipbuilding depended. Their solution, a transporter bridge, was opened in 1893, damaged during the Civil War (1936–39) and rebuilt in 1941. The bridge, whose iron structure is reminiscent of the Eiffel Tower, can also be crossed by the walkway on top, which affords splendid views of Portugalete, Neguri's wealthy neighbour in Getxo, the port and Abra bay. A new gondola was unveiled in 1999, the fifth in the bridge's history; its predecessors together had carried an estimated 650 million people and had made the equivalent of 31 round-the-world journeys. The gondola holds 6 cars and 200 passengers; per-person and per-car charges apply.

The gondola takes 90 seconds to cross and does so every eight minutes. If you have a head for heights, take the panoramic lift and walk across (it's enclosed and safe). ❸ Barria 3, Las Arenas (Getxo) ❶ 944 801 012 Ⓦ www.puente-colgante.com

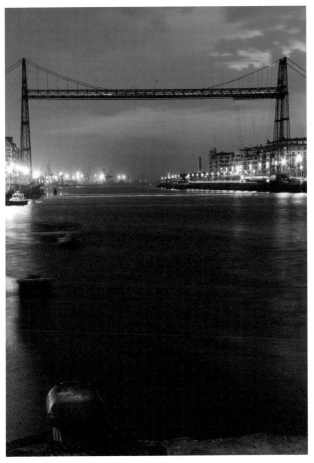

◆ Bilbao's transporter bridge, a World Heritage Site

ⓔ promociones@puente-colgante.com  ⓛ 24 hours daily
ⓝ Metro: from Bilbao to Portugalete or Las Arenas (Getxo)

### San Mamés Stadium

Bilbao's 'cathedral of football' was erected in 1952 on the site
of one dating back to 1913, 15 years after the foundation of
the Athletic Bilbao club (or *los leones*, the Lions, as they are
known locally). It was remodelled for the 1982 World Cup.
ⓐ C/Felipe Serrate  ⓣ 944 240 877  ⓦ www.athletic-club.net
ⓝ Metro/Tram: San Mamés

### Teatro Campos Elíseos

This architecturally over-the-top theatre – an unmissable Art
Nouveau tour de force designed by Alfredo Acebal and Jean Baptiste
Darroguy – was opened in 1902 in an area called the Campos Elíseos
(Elysian Fields). Locals refer to it as *la bombonera* (the chocolate box).
ⓐ C/Bertendona 5  ⓝ Metro/Tram: Abando

## CULTURE

### Ayuntamiento (town hall)

The town hall's style, like that of the Bidebarrieta City Library
(see page 66), is eclectic. It was built at the end of the 19th century
by Joaquín Rucoba, who took references from the classicist style of
the Third French Republic. Opposite the town hall, on a small square
that marks the beginning of the Paseo Campo Volantín, is Jorge
Oteiza's sculpture, *The Ovoid Variation of the De-occupation of the
Sphere*, which represents the artist's concern with emptiness.
ⓐ Pl. Ernesto Erkoreka  ⓝ Metro: Abando

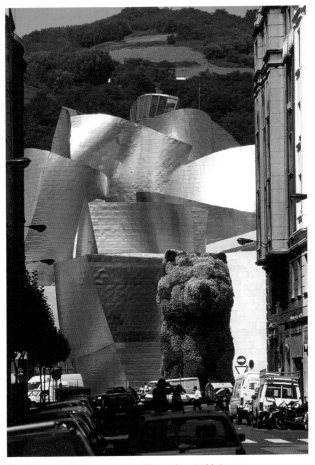

◆ *The Guggenheim is guarded by Jeff Koons' irresistible* Puppy

### *GUERNICA*

The painting that has stirred up the most controversy at the Bilbao Guggenheim is the one that isn't there: Pablo Picasso's *Guernica*, painted in response to the bombing of the town of the same name in 1937 by German bombers allied with Franco's Nationalists. The painting's symbolic importance to the Basques is huge: there was great jockeying to be the host of this famous work of art and much disappointment when the painting went to the Reina Sofía art gallery in Madrid. Basques have been demanding the return of this evocative piece of art ever since.

### Bilbao Guggenheim Museum

The most famous cultural institution in the city is the Bilbao Guggenheim Museum, which was built in 1997 and played a huge role in the revitalisation of the cultural landscape of the city. The ambitious project to bring part of the famous New York museum's collection to Bilbao began in 1991, when representatives of the Basque regional government approached the Solomon R Guggenheim Foundation with their plan to regenerate Bilbao and the Basque Country. The Trustees of the Foundation welcomed the proposal warmly, as it complemented their own plans for long-term international development to extend the collection. In its first year, the Bilbao Guggenheim received over a million visitors.

The truly extraordinary building was designed by Canadian Frank Gehry and is a fine manifestation of his 'architecture is art' philosophy, mixing form and function to impressive effect. The giant sculpture with sensuous titanium curves is sometimes likened to a vast shimmering flower. Titanium was chosen as the building material to achieve a warm-looking surface that would glow even on an overcast or rainy day. Walk to the Puente de la Salve for a great vantage point from which to admire this remarkable piece of architecture.

*Puppy*, Jeff Koons' flower sculpture, stands by the main entrance. This huge mountain of flowers has been adopted as an emblem of the city and you'll find *Puppy* souvenirs hard to avoid. Inside, there is a vast, airy and light atrium, leading to three floors of superb art from the 20th century. American sculptor Richard Serra's minimalist work aims to introduce the viewers to large-scale sculptures. Near the river is Louise Bourgeois' huge bronze sculpture *Maman*, which forms part of her Spider series, representing maternity.

Free guided tours in English (limited to 20 people subject to availability – reserve places in advance). The popularity of this museum is phenomenal, so be prepared for queues, especially at the weekend. There's a shop and café-bar on the first floor, and a good restaurant where you can try 'new Basque' cooking.
ⓐ Av. Abandoibarra 2 ⓣ 944 359 080; guided tour reservation 10.00–20.00 Tues–Sun ⓦ www.guggenheim-bilbao.es
ⓛ 10.00–20.00 Tues–Sun; also open Mon in July & Aug. Closed 25 Dec & 1 Jan ⓜ Metro: Moyúa; Tram: Guggenheim; Bilbobus: 1, 10, 13, 18 to Plaza del Museo ⓘ Admission charge

## Museo de Arte Sacro (Museum of Sacred Art)

This museum occupies the former Convento de la Encarnación, which was founded in 1515. Here you will find religious art and craft dating back to the 12th century, along with sculptures and paintings by Basque artists, and a huge collection of silverware from Spain and its former colonies in the Americas. ⓐ Pl. de la Encarnación 9

🕐 10.30–13.30, 16.00–19.00 Tues–Sat, 10.30–13.20 Sun, closed Mon
ℹ️ Admission charge (Thur free) 🚊 Tram: Atxuri

## Museo de Bellas Artes (Fine Arts Museum)

This gallery, at the end of Parque de Doña Casilda de Iturrizar, tends to be overshadowed by its more famous neighbour, the Guggenheim, but don't let this deter you. Art lovers will find it well worth a visit, with its collection of works by well-known masters, as well as pieces by more modern artists.

More than 300 works are on show from Romanesque pieces to 20th-century avant-garde, arranged in chronological order, and

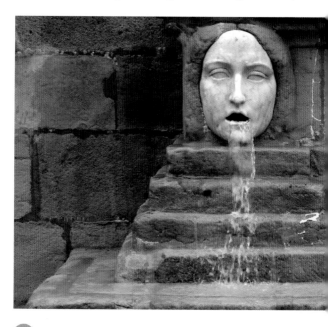

the museum also hosts some interesting temporary exhibitions. You'll find works spanning the 12th to the 20th centuries by Goya, El Greco, Zurbaran, Rivera, Van Dyck, Gauguin and Bacon; Basque artists, including Zuloaga and Oteiza, are also well represented. There's a restaurant and a bar with good views. ❸ Pl. del Museo ❶ 944 396 060 ⓦ www.museobilbao.com ⏰ 10.00–20.00 Tues–Sun, closed Mon ⓜ Metro: Moyúa; Tram: Abandoibarra; Bilbobus: 1, 10, 13, 18 to Plaza del Museo ❶ Admission charge (free on Wed); combined ticket with Guggenheim €13.50

● *Decorative heads on a fountain in central Bilbao*

### Museo Marítimo (Maritime Museum)

The Ría de Bilbao Maritime Museum is located in the docks of the old Euskalduna shipyard, a stone's throw away from the Guggenheim and the Fine Arts Museum. It explores Bilbao's long association with the sea and shipbuilding. The permanent exhibition shows the evolution and heritage of Bilbao's estuary as a seaport and shipyard. Outside there is a dock area with old fishing boats on display. ⓐ Muelle Ramón de la Sota 1 ⓣ 902 131 000 ⓦ www.museomaritimobilbao.org ⓛ 10.00–20.00 Tues–Sun, closed Mon (summer); Tues–Fri 10.00–18.00, Sat & Sun 10.00–20.00, closed Mon (winter) ⓝ Metro: Sabino Arana; Tram: Euskalduna

## RETAIL THERAPY

The majority of Bilbao's department stores can be found on the Gran Vía. The big designer names, such as Gucci and Calvin Klein, are also found along here. Don't forget the gift shop at the Guggenheim and the Fine Arts Museum; both have a big selection of items themed around their respective collections.

**La Casa del Libro** This bookshop has an extensive range of books and maps, including English-language books. ⓐ Colón de Larreátegui 41 ⓣ 902 026 409 ⓦ www.casadellibro.com ⓛ 09.30–21.30 Mon–Sat, 11.30–15.00, 16.30–21.30 Sun ⓝ Metro/Tram: Abando

**El Corte Inglés** The Bilbao branch of this renowned Spanish department store chain should satisfy virtually all your shopping needs, from luxury to everyday items. ⓐ Gran Vía 7–9 ⓣ 944 253 500 ⓦ www.elcorteingles.es ⓛ 10.00–21.00 Mon–Sat, closed Sun ⓝ Metro/Tram: Abando

**For** Men and women's clothes, mainly casualwear, made with high-quality fabrics. ⓐ Gran Vía 22 ⓣ 944 356 302 ⓦ www.for.es ⓛ 10.00–20.30 Mon–Sat, closed Sun ⓝ Metro/Tram: Abando

**Zubiarte** Exclusive design and avant-garde architecture converge at this upmarket shopping centre with more than 70 shops. ⓐ Lehendakari Leizaola 2 ⓣ 944 277 380 ⓦ www.zubiarte.com ⓛ 10.00–22.00 daily (restaurants close later) ⓝ Tram: Abandoibarra

## TAKING A BREAK

Whichever part of the modern city you visit, you won't need much help in finding a café or bar where you can relax over a coffee or a drink (see map pages 56–7).

**Garibolo £** ❶ Cosy vegetarian restaurant with friendly staff. ⓐ C/Fernández del Campo 7 ⓣ 944 223 255 ⓛ 13.00–16.00, 21.00–23.00 Mon–Sat, closed Sun ⓝ Metro: Moyúa

**Abaroa ££** ❷ A restaurant with a big window to look out at the Museo de Bellas Artes. Traditional Basque cuisine. ⓐ Pl. del Museo 3 ⓣ 944 249 107 ⓦ www.abaroa.net ⓝ Metro: Moyúa

**Café Bar Iruña ££** ❸ Dating from 1903, with a Moorish-style interior décor of coloured ceramic tiles, this remains a popular meeting point for a young white-collar crowd, and gets busy from early morning until late into the night. Come for breakfast, lunch or evening drinks, when the music is turned up. ⓐ Jardines de Albia 5 ⓣ 944 237 021 ⓛ 07.00–02.00 Mon–Fri, 09.00–02.00 Sat, 12.00–01.00 Sun ⓝ Metro/Tram: Abando

◐ The Guggenheim has first-class catering facilities

**Kikara ££** ❹ Two-floor restaurant near the Guggenheim serving accomplished modern cuisine at reasonable prices. ⓐ C/Iparraguirre 23 ❶ 944 236 840 ❷ 12.00–24.00 Mon–Thur, 12.00–02.00 Fri & Sat, closed Sun ⓝ Metro: Moyúa

**La Granja ££** ❺ One of the oldest cafés in the city, opened in 1926 and known for its elegant, old-fashioned feel. ⓐ Pl. Circular 3 ❶ 944 230 813 ❷ 07.00–23.00 Mon–Fri, 10.00–02.30 Sat, closed Sun ⓝ Metro/Tram: Abando

## AFTER DARK

### RESTAURANTS

**Casa Vasca ££** ❻ Value-for-money traditional Basque cuisine in the Deusto district. Try the spicy cod dish *bacalao al pil pil*, and for dessert *arroz con leche* (rice pudding). It's also a patisserie – try the delicious toasted croissants. ⓐ Av. Lehendakari Aguirre 13 ❶ 944 483 980 ⓦ www.casavasca.com ❷ 13.00–15.30, 21.00–23.00 daily ⓝ Metro: Deusto

**La Taberna del Sur de Deusto ££** ❼ Get a taste of southern Spain in this Andalusian-style *taberna*, which is decorated with flamenco paraphernalia. The menu features fried fish, seafood from Huelva, Serrano (dry-cured) ham and other southern delicacies. ⓐ C/Heliodoro de la Torre 2 ❶ 944 751 569 ⓦ www.tabernadelsurdedeusto.com ❷ 12.00–16.30, 20.00–23.00 Mon–Thur, 12.00–16.30, 20.00–24.00 Fri–Sat, closed Sun ⓝ Metro: Deusto

**Mina ££** ❽ Located opposite Mercado de la Ribera, with big windows looking out over the river bank, this restaurant decked

out in wood and stone has a warm feel. The menu is seasonal.
ⓐ Muelle Marzana ☎ 944 795 938 🕐 13.00–16.00, 20.00–23.00
Wed–Sat. Closed Mon, Tues & Sun evening Ⓝ Tram: Ribera

**Nicolás ££** ❾ Another good bet for traditional Basque dishes,
especially fish, such as *bacalao* (salted cod) and *merluza* (hake).
The bar also offers *pintxos*. ⓐ C/Ledesma 10 ☎ 944 240 737
🕐 Daily except Sun evening Ⓝ Metro/Tram: Abando

**Guria £££** ❿ A well-established restaurant offering upmarket
versions of authentic Basque dishes in elegant surroundings.
*Surtidos de bacalao* (salted cod) is the chef's speciality. ⓐ Gran Vía 66
☎ 944 415 780 Ⓦ www.restauranteguria.com 🕐 Daily except Sun
evening Ⓝ Metro: Moyúa

**Zortziko £££** ⓫ A top-of-the-range restaurant in a historic setting.
House dishes include roast fillet of grouper with truffle, scallops,
and vegetables with truffle oil. ⓐ Alameda Mazarredo 17 ☎ 944 239
743 Ⓦ www.zortziko.es 🕐 Lunch & dinner Tues–Sat, closed Mon &
Sun Ⓝ Metro: Abando; Tram: Uribitarte

## CLUBS & BARS

Central Bilbao has an abundance of clubs catering to all musical
tastes. The area around Calle Mazarredo is a very popular
night-time haunt, as are the pubs found in the Urquijo *galerías*
(passageways). Ledesma and Licenciado Poza are good for bar-
hopping, where the in-drink is *kalimotxo* (coke and red wine,
invented by locals more than 30 years ago). Local favourites include
La Granja and Iruña.

**Alambique** The rather romantic daytime atmosphere of this bar – a good place to come for breakfast – changes dramatically at night when it gets packed with people. Music varies from jazz to lounge. ⓐ C/Alameda de Urquijo 37 ❶ 044 434 188 ◐ 08.00–24.00 Mon–Thur, 08.00–01.00 Fri–Sat, closed Sun Ⓝ Metro: Moyúa

**Azkena** Specialises in live music, from reggae to rock. ⓐ C/Ibañez de Bilbao 26 Ⓦ www.azkena.com Ⓝ Metro/Tram: Abando

**Bar Poza 40** A lively place (with Wi-Fi) to join the locals watching Athletic de Bilbao on a big TV screen. ⓐ C/Licenciado Poza 40 ❶ 944 416 639 ◐ 08.00–24.00 daily Ⓝ Metro: Indautxu

**Cotton Club** Monthly live concerts. ⓐ C/Gregorio de la Revilla 25 ❶ 944 104 951 ◐ 20.30–03.00 Mon–Thur, 20.30–06.00 Fri–Sat, closed Sun Ⓝ Metro: Indautxu

**El Salero** Modern, elegant place with white décor and warm lighting. It's a restaurant, a bar and a place to relax. ⓐ C/Manuel Allende 5 ❶ 944 103 552 Ⓝ Metro: Indautxu

**Mystik** In the afternoon this is the perfect place for a drink or a coffee. At night the temperature and the volume of the music rise. ⓐ C/Ercilla 1 ❶ 944 236 342 ◐ 14.00–04.00 Mon–Thur, 14.00–05.00 Fri–Sat, closed Sun Ⓝ Metro: Moyúa

**Sala Crystal** Dance the night away in this disco playing a good selection of eclectic music. ⓐ Pl. de Venezuela 1 ❶ 944 242 508 ◐ 23.00–04.00 daily Ⓝ Metro: Abando

**Santana 27** The biggest dance club in town, with four venues, each with different music. It also hosts concerts. C/Santa Ana M Bolueta www.santana27.com Metro: Bolueta

**Stromboli** DJ sessions, art exhibitions and live performances make this easy-going central bar in the centre popular. Come for breakfast, a drink or a snack. C/General Concha 12 944 051 872 10.30–01.00 Mon–Thur, Sun, 10.30–03.00 Fri & Sat Metro: Moyúa

**Wicklow Arms** This small bar on Plaza Campuzano is where English-speaking expats in Bilbao get together on Wednesdays, Thursdays and Fridays. It serves the best Guinness in town. C/Rodriguez Arias 70 944 425 148 12.00–02.00 daily Metro: Moyúa

**Witch Café Pub** This café plays alternative and international music mixed in with more predictable rock and pop. Cosme Echevarrieta 4 944 241 023 10.00–04.00 Mon–Sat Metro: Moyúa

---

● *Explore the ruggedly beautiful Basque coast*

# OUT OF TOWN
trips

# San Sebastián

San Sebastián, or Donostia, as the Basques call it, is one of the most delightful towns in northern Spain, with an ideal location on the beautiful Bahía de la Concha with its golden beaches. It has a French feel, and the aptly named Centro Romántico consists of splendid old buildings. There are also a number of pleasant parks around the city. **Tourist office** ⓐ Oficina de Turismo, Teatro Victoria Eugenia, Boulevard 8 ❶ 943 481 166 Ⓦ www.sansebastianturismo.com ❶ 09.00–13.30, 15.30–19.00 Mon–Thur, 09.30–19.00 Fri–Sat, 10.00–14.00 Sun Ⓝ Bus: 21, 26, 28

## GETTING THERE

Up to three Euskotren (Ⓦ www.euskotren.es) trains an hour depart from Estación Atxuri in Bilbao for San Sebastián (Donostia). You may find it easier to catch the metro from the centre of Bilbao to the suburban Bolueta station and catch the train from there. Or take the bus, which is quicker and more frequent. Buses from Bilbao's Termibus terminal (Ⓝ Metro/Tram: San Mamés) take only 1 hour and 10 minutes and leave every hour. By car it's an easy journey along the A8 *autopista* (motorway) – approximately 100 km (60 miles).

## SIGHTS & ATTRACTIONS

The Parte Vieja is the old part of the town, by the sea and overlooked by Monte Urgull, with its narrow streets, the Parque de Alderdi Eder and a huge Ayuntamiento (town hall) dating from the 19th century.

The Playa de la Concha is San Sebastián's biggest beach and it forms a golden swathe of sand, with delights such as the promenade of the Paseo de la Concha and the Palacio Miramar Maria Cristina, originally built as a summer house for the Spanish royal family.

A sculpture by Eduardo Chillida (see page 108) – *Peine de los Vientos*, or *Comb of the Winds* – stands by the shore, just beyond the beach; it comprises a number of terraces built into rocks with cast-iron adornments, where the wind sweeps in from the sea.

Take the funicular ride from the end of the beach, where at the top you will be treated to magnificent views over the town, the Bay of Biscay and the mountains of Cantabria in the distance.

### Aquarium

Children especially will love this attraction, which has a large array of marine creatures on display. An underwater glass corridor under the main tank allows you to get up close and personal with the stars of the show, the sharks Txuri and Urdin. A skeleton of a whale and model ships are also on view.

ⓐ Pl. Carlos Blasco de Imaz ❶ 943 440 099 Ⓦ www.aquariumss.com
🕓 10.00–19.00 Mon–Fri, 10.00–20.00 Sat & Sun (closes later in summer) ❶ Admission charge

### Basílica Santa María del Coro

Situated on the Vía Coro, this 18th-century church is a mixture of Baroque and neoclassical styles. San Sebastián himself is depicted in a sculpture on the façade and there are a number of rococo objects.

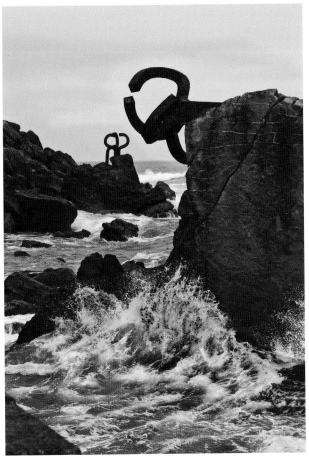

🔺 *Eduardo Chillida's* Comb of the Winds *sculpture*

### CALLE 31 DE AGOSTO

31 August 1813 was a disastrous day in the history of San Sebastián. When the Duke of Wellington's Anglo-Portuguese army captured the city from the French in the Napoleonic Wars, the town was ransacked and torched (despite the fact that the Spanish were supposed to be on the same side as the British). Only the churches of San Vicente and Santa Maria and a few of the houses in the streets between were left standing. The fateful day is remembered every 31 August, when candles are lit in the balconies of this street.

### Catedral del Buen Pastor (Cathedral of the Good Shepherd)

The 75-m (250-ft) spire of this atmospheric neo-Gothic cathedral is visible throughout the old town. Finished in the late 19th century, the cathedral is situated in a square with relaxing gardens.

### Monte Igeldo

Perched above the beach at Ondarreta to the east of the city centre, Monte Igeldo (Igueldo in Spanish) has over 6 sq km (2½ sq miles) of hilly parkland and is close to the rocky northern coastline. The quiet roads are ideal for walking and cycling. In contrast to the peaceful natural beauty, there's a funfair at the top of the hill, which can be reached from Ondarreta beach by a funicular railway. Funicular Ⓦ www.monteigueldo.es Ⓛ 10.00–22.00 daily (summer); closed Wed (winter)

### Monte Urgull and Castillo Santa Cruz de la Mota

A network of steep paths and steps climbs the wooded headland of Monte Urgull behind the port and aquarium, before eventually

◆ *San Sebastian has centre stage on the façade of Santa Maria del Coro*

reaching the castle (which houses a history museum). From the battlements, there are great views over the city and the bay.

### Museo Chillida-Leku

Located 8 km (5 miles) out of town, this museum is dedicated to the work of Eduardo Chillida (1924–2002), a leading sculptor of the Escuela Vasca (Basque School), a movement that is rooted in traditional Basque culture. Chillida restored this 16th-century farmhouse and financed the museum himself as a place to display his huge sculptures made from granite and iron, which are set in 12 ha (30 acres) of lawn and woodland. ⓐ Jáuregui 66 ⓣ 943 336 006 ⓦ www.eduardo-chillida.com ⓛ 10.30–20.00 Mon–Sat, 10.30–15.00 Sun (summer); 10.30–15.00 Wed–Mon, closed Tues (winter)

### Museo Naval (Ship Museum)

This museum displays the long and interesting seafaring history of the Basques. It also highlights the important role that shipbuilding played in the development of the city. The museum is housed in the late 18th-century Consular Warehouse situated behind the port, in a building that was previously used as a guildhall. ⓐ Paseo del Muelle 24 ⓣ 943 430 051 ⓛ 10.00–13.30, 16.00–19.30 Tues–Sat, 11.00–14.00 Sun, closed Mon ⓘ Admission charge

### Museo San Telmo

This museum is located in an ancient Dominican monastery, dating back to the 16th century. A series of renovations has restored much of the church and cloisters, and the building has come to be regarded as a Basque national monument. There is a permanent exhibition on traditional Basque lifestyle, and also regular

temporary exhibitions. The golden murals by Josep Maria Sert, a Catalan artist, depict the history of the Basques. ❸ Pl. Zuloaga
❶ 943 481 580 Ⓦ www.museosantelmo.com
🕐 Closed for refurbishment until spring 2011

## Plaza de la Constitución

Known to the locals as 'Consti', this square is the focal point of the old town. It was once used as a bullring and the balconies overlooking the square were rented out to spectators. It is a hub of activity with busy terrace bars and a key party spot, especially during the festivals of Santo Tomás in December and San Sebastián in January.

## Puente de Maria Cristina

Inspired by the Pont Alexander III in Paris, the bridge is richly decorated with dragons, maritime scenes and coats of arms.

## Tabacalera

The new International Contemporary Culture Centre in San Sebastián is housed in a former tobacco factory, and the building's industrial aesthetics have been well preserved. It explores cinema, television, contemporary art, design, science and gastronomy. Science and techonology are key fields, and the aim is to create a space in which culture, science and technology can interact. The factory took 25 years to complete and was in use for over 90 years, employing around a thousand workers at its peak. The tobacco company was privatised and in 2003 the factory was closed down.
❸ C/Duque de Mandas 52 ❶ 943 011 311 Ⓦ www.tabacalera.eu
🕐 Various depending on activity

## TAKING A BREAK

You can get tasty tapas and seafood in most of the cafés and bars around the Parte Vieja. But finding a more substantial meal won't be a problem: San Sebastián has several high-quality restaurants, some of them rated among the best in Spain.

**Ubarrechena £** This is one of the cheapest places to dine in the old town and is accordingly popular with tourists and the locals. ⓐ C/del Puerto 16 ⓣ 943 425 794 ⓛ Daily

**Beti Jai ££** This restaurant is one the best seafood restaurants in town, with seafood salads a speciality; meat and other dishes also served. ⓐ C/Fermín Calbetón 22 ⓣ 943 427 737 ⓦ www.betijai.com ⓛ Lunch & dinner Mon, Wed–Sun; closed Tues

**Casa Urola ££** This is a splendid restaurant with a busy bar and a good-value *menú del día*. Popular. ⓐ C/Fermín Calbetón 20 ⓣ 943 423 424 ⓦ www.restauranteurola.com ⓛ Lunch & dinner Thur–Tues, closed Sun evening and all day Wed

## SPORT & RELAXATION

### CYCLING

As an alternative to exploring the city on foot, it's well worth considering hiring a bike. Keep a watchful eye out for pedestrians, however, as walkers also use the cycle lanes. You can hire cycles and get information on routes from the following companies:
**Bici Rent Donosti** ⓐ Av. de la Zurriola 22 ⓣ 639 016 013
**Grosjean Center** ⓐ Peña y Goñi 3 ⓣ 943 288 940

△ *A sign of good seafood*

## DAY TRIPS/EXCURSIONS/GUIDED VISITS

**Begi Bistan** Organises guided cultural visits, walks and nature trips – including whale-watching boat trips. Activities are normally on Saturday or Sunday. Prices range from €12–100. ❶ 657 794 677 ⓦ www.begi-bistan.com

## TOURIST TRAIN

**Txu-Txu** The train runs along La Concha beach to Ondarreta, taking in the Palacio de Miramar and, on its way back, the cathedral, the Teatro Victoria Eugenia and the Ayuntamiento. Departures are every 30 minutes and the journey takes approximately 40 minutes. ❶ 943 422 973 ⓛ 10.00–21.00 daily (summer); 11.00–14.00, 15.00–19.00 (winter)

## BOAT TRIPS

**Ciudad de San Sebastian Catamaran** Departing from the Paseo del Muelle (near the Museo Naval), this vessel offers excursions around La Concha Bay, passing the mouth of the Urumea River, Zurriola beach, Monte Igueldo, Monte Urgull, Peine de los Vientos and the Isla de Santa Clara, a small island off La Concha Bay. On the way back it passes along the beaches of Ondarreta and La Concha. The journey takes 30 minutes and requires a minimum of ten passengers. Tickets are €8 (adults) and €4 (children). ❶ 607 201155 ⓦ www.ciudadsansebastian.com ⓛ Departures at 12.30, 16.00, 17.00 & 18.00 Mon–Fri, also 19.00 Sat & Sun

**Ferries to Isla de Santa Clara** These passenger ferries run from June–September in good weather only. ❶ 943 000 450

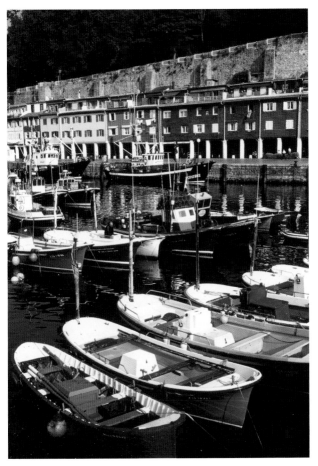

◆ San Sebastián's fishing harbour is close to the old fortifications

## ACCOMMODATION

San Sebastián is not a cheap place to stay. It's very popular with tourists year round; French tourists hop over for the weekend, or even just for a night out. The least expensive option is a *hostal*.

**Pensión Urgull £** Lovely, cheap option with nicely decorated and well-looked-after rooms. Pleasant views. ⓐ C/Esterlines 10 ⓣ 943 430 047

**Hotel Monte Ulia ££** Located in a quiet part of San Sebastián, just four minutes' walk from Gros beach. Neat rooms, many with balconies, a restaurant and free parking. ⓐ Alcalde Jose Elosegi 21 ⓣ 943 326 767 ⓦ www.hotelmonteulia.com ⓔ contacto@hotelmonteulia.com ⓝ Bus: 13

**Pensión Aldamar ££** Located on the Bulevar, facing the Teatro Victoria Eugenia and a stone's throw from the beach, this pension has ten pleasant en-suite bedrooms with free Wi-Fi access. ⓐ C/Aldamar 2 ⓣ 943 430 143 ⓕ 943 423 695 ⓦ www.pensionaldamar.com

**Pensión Alemana ££** This pleasant B&B is situated near the cathedral. The rooms are en-suite. ⓐ C/San Martin 53 ⓣ 943 462 544 ⓦ www.pensionalemana.com

**Hostal Parma £££** Located by the Parte Vieja and Paseo Nuevo; some rooms have sea views. ⓐ Paseo de Salamanca 10 ⓣ 943 428 893 ⓦ www.hotelparma.com

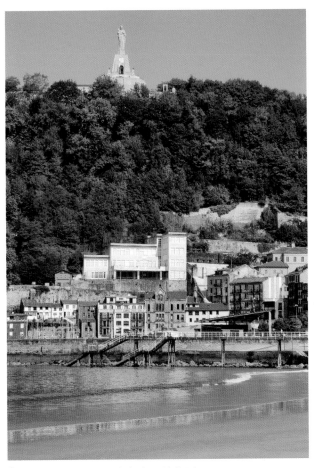

● *Monte Urgull rises above the harbourside hotels*

# Vitoria

Vitoria (Gasteiz in the Basque language) is the capital of rural Alava and the seat of the autonomous Basque Parliament. Vitoria flourished in the Renaissance, which left its mark by way of the beautiful churches and palaces. The town was also hit hard by wars, such as the Peninsular War, and it was here, in 1813, that Wellington defeated Napoleon's forces in one of his most celebrated victories. However, by the late 19th century Vitoria was once again flourishing. Despite its troubled history, the city has been impressively preserved.
**Tourist office** ❷ Pl. General Loma ❶ 945 161 598
Ⓦ www.vitoria-gasteiz.org Ⓛ 10.00–19.00 Mon–Sat, 11.00–14.00 Sun

## GETTING THERE

RENFE trains from Bilbao's Estación Abando go to Miranda de Ebro, where you change to catch a main-line train to Vitoria. The total journey time is a little over 3 hours. Vitoria's RENFE station is on the south side of the city. Buses from Bilbao's Termibus station leave for Vitoria every hour, and take 1 hour. The bus station in Vitoria is on Calle de Los Herrán.

## SIGHTS & ATTRACTIONS

The Casco Viejo, or old town, consisting of a series of concentric streets, is Gothic in character. These days it's a little run-down in parts but it has some attractive mansions and churches. The porticoed Plaza de España is lovely and a popular place to gather for drinks or a leisurely stroll, particularly in the early evening. Plaza de la Virgen Blanca, fringed by ancient houses, is a medieval square in the

oldest part of town. The San Miguel church dates from the 14th century and is worth a visit. Artium, the Basque Museum of Contemporary Art, has permanent and temporary exhibitions.

### Casa del Cordón

This 14th-century Gothic tower is immediately adjacent to a 15th-century palace. The star-studded dome of the palace is one of the last remaining examples of Gothic decorative art to be found in the region. ⓐ C/Cuchillería 24

### Catedral de la María Inmaculada

This curious building in the Parque de la Florida was constructed at the outset of the 20th century in a medieval Gothic-esque style, using historic building methods. It also houses the Diocesan Museum of Sacred Art (see page 122). ⓐ C/Monseñor Cadena y Eleta

### Catedral de Santa María

This fine old Gothic church is a source of great pride to the city – and indeed to the whole of Spain. It gave Vitoria a major feather in its cap by winning the Europa Nostra prize, the European Union's highest award for conservation. Visitors to the cathedral are encouraged to take a look at the ongoing restoration and to learn about the techniques used to preserve the architecture of the building. The cathedral has an exquisitely carved western doorway and a gallery built of stone around the naves; the aisles have tombs dating from medieval times. ⓐ C/Cuchillería

### Church of San Miguel

This 14th-century Gothic church houses a number of interesting historic artefacts, including a statue of the patron saint of the city

◆ The interior of the newly restored Catedral de Santa María

## THE BATTLE OF VITORIA

On 21 June 1813, in the countryside to the north and west of Vitoria, the Duke of Wellington's army confronted their French adversaries under Joseph Bonaparte, brother of the Emperor Napoleon. The fighting was intense and it was only after a long and desperate struggle that the French were defeated, leading to the capture of Vitoria by the allies. As was to happen also in San Sebastián, the victorious troops could not be restrained from looting the town afterwards. The human cost of the battle was the loss of 13,000 men, but the defeat effectively ended the French occupation of Spain and signalled the beginning of the end of French supremacy in Europe. The composer Beethoven wrote a symphony called *Wellington's Victory* to commemorate the battle. On a less elevated note, the British 14th Hussars captured a silver chamber pot from Joseph Bonaparte's baggage train. The pot is used to this day by the modern-day descendants of the regiment to make champagne toasts.

and, in the apse, the symbolic Machete Vitoriana, before which every new attorney general to the city swore an oath before taking office. The building also boasts a 17th-century altar by Gregorio Fernández and nine chapels. ⓐ Pl. de la Virgen Blanca ⓛ Daily

### Church of San Pedro

Constructed at the end of the 13th century, this church, after the cathedral, is the oldest in Vitoria, and has some interesting sculptures inside. ⓐ C/Fundadora de las Servias de Jesús 2

## Los Arquillos

When Vitoria began to expand in the late 18th century, the city architects were faced with bridging the gap between the medieval town and the land that was to be developed. Their solution was to build Los Arquillos. These beautiful colonnades were constructed between 1787 and 1802. The first section runs alongside the Cuesta de San Francisco and the second along the Church of San Miguel. With the Plaza España, they represent the finest examples of neoclassical architecture in the Basque Country.

## Plaza de España

This fine example of 18th-century neoclassical architecture, with an impressive façade, was the result of the first major expansion of the city from its medieval core.

## Plaza de la Virgen Blanca

A popular meeting point, this square is overlooked by the Church of San Vicente, which bears more than a passing resemblance to the Catedral Santa María. Its 15th-century Gothic tower offers great panoramic views of Vitoria. The square hosts the opening of the Fiesta de la Virgen in August, the city's biggest event, when the descent of mythical figure Celedón across the plaza marks the beginning of the celebrations (see page 124).

## CULTURE

### Centro Museo Vasco de Arte Contemporáneo (Basque Museum of Contemporary Art)

This museum, designed by a local architect, displays an intriguing array of over 1,600 paintings, drawings, photographs and sculptures from contemporary artists, as well as temporary exhibitions of more recent art. ❸ C/Francia 24 Ⓦ www.artium.org Ⓛ 11.00–14.00, 17.00–20.00 Tues–Thur, 11.00–14.00, 16.00–21.00 Fri–Sun, closed Mon

### Museo Arqueológico (Archaeological Museum)

The museum has a collection of finds from prehistoric to medieval times, with artefacts from the Bronze Age, Iron Age and the Roman era on display. ❸ C/Cuchillería 54 Ⓛ 10.00–14.00, 16.00–18.30 Tues–Fri, 10.00–14.00 Sat, 11.00–14.00 Sun, closed Mon

### Museo de Bellas Artes (Fine Arts Museum)

This gallery is contained in a wonderfully restored house built in the Renaissance Revival style of the early 20th century. It has a well-laid-out display of early art up to the time of Zuloaga, Amárica and Maeztu. It also has a decent collection of paintings by contemporary Spanish and Basque artists, the latter being especially well represented.

A sizeable collection of work is from the first Basque School of the mid-19th century, which shows 'costumbrista' pictures, paintings of everyday life that were very typical of the time. Contemporary Spanish art from 1950 to the present day forms the most extensive collection in the museum. ❸ Paseo Fray Francisco de Vitoria 8 Ⓛ 10.00–14.00, 16.00–18.30 Tues–Fri, 10.00–14.00, 17.00–20.00 Sat, 11.00–14.00 Sun, closed Mon

### Museo Diocesano de Arte Sacro (Diocesan Museum of Sacred Art)

Located in the Catedral de la María Inmaculada, this museum harbours a collection of religious treasures from the likes of Ribera, Luca Giordano and El Greco. ❸ C/Monseñor Cadena y Eleta Ⓛ 10.00–14.00, 16.00–18.30 Tues–Sat, 11.00–14.00 Sun, closed Mon

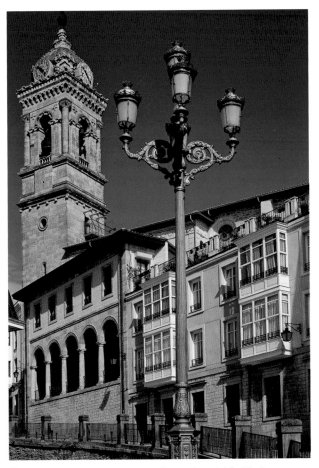

La Plaza de la Virgen Blanca is a popular meeting point for Vitorians

**t** 945 151 259 **w** www.lacasadelosarquillos.com
**e** info@lacasadelosarquillos.com

**Almoneda £££** This is a recently refurbished, family-run hotel offering straightforward, elegant rooms with amenities.
**a** C/Florida 7 **t** 945 154 084 **w** www.hotelalmoneda.com
**e** information@hotelalmoneda.com

**Hotel Silken Ciudad de Victoria £££** An opulent 4-star hotel in the heart of the city, offering everything expected of a high-end hotel.
**a** Portal de Castilla 8 **t** 945 141 100 **f** 945 143 616
**w** www.hoteles-silken.com

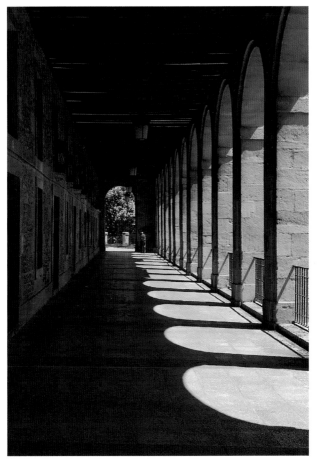

● *The beautiful colonnades of Vitoria's neoclassical Arquillos*

# The Costa Vasca

This coastal route taking you from Bilbao to San Sebastián affords some splendid scenery, with cliffs and great, wild sea views. Working fishing villages with some fine beaches (including Pedernales and Mundaka, which are well known for surfing) are dotted along this stretch of coast.

A less romantic and more troubled spot is Lemoiz, which saw mass protests against the building of a nuclear reactor in the 1970s and 1980s – the project was abandoned in the early 1990s.

### SOPELANA

A haunt of surfers and hang-gliders with breathtaking coastal scenery. It's also a popular spot to just hang out on the beach.

### PLENTZIA

A traditional fishing port, Plentzia has successfully reconciled its past with the modern requirements of watersport enthusiasts. It's a great place just to relax, wander the streets and watch the harbour life. The Museo Plasentia de Butrón houses an interesting collection of maritime artefacts. For a good meal here, try:

**Gurea ££** This restaurant and *asador* serves traditional Basque dishes. ➌ Pl. Txoa 6 ❶ 946 770 288 ❺ 13.00–16.00, 21.00–24.00 daily

### GATIKA

You pass the fairytale-style Castillo de Butrón on the way from Plentzia to Mungia. Built originally in the 11th century, it had a makeover in the 19th century, and is an impressive sight. ❶ Closed to the public, but has an interesting garden that can be visited

## GORLIZ

Another very popular beach, the main landmark in Gorliz is the lighthouse, a great vantage point for ocean views. You can also explore the small 18th-century fort.

## BAKIO

Bakio's two main claims to fame are *txakoli* and surf. *Txakoli* is a tart green wine made from a blend of local grape varietals and was very popular in the 16th century. It is once again gaining popularity among the Basques, and you can visit the wineries in the valley inland from the bay. The 6-km (4-mile) long beach at Bakio is becoming something of a mecca for surfers. Bakio has several restaurants offering hearty Basque food and good views.

**Gotzon ££** ⓐ C/Bentalde 133 ❶ 946 194 043
**Eneperi £££** ⓐ C/Gibelorratzagako San Pelaio ❶ 946 194 065
ⓦ www.eneperi.com

If you plan to stay in Bakio, try:
**Hotel Arimune ££** Centrally located on the beach, this is an attractively quaint hotel with terraces overlooking the sea.
ⓐ C/Bentalde 95 ❶ 946 194 022

## SAN JUAN DE GAZTELUGATXE

This rocky promontory formed a starting point of the medieval pilgrimage route of St James to the holy shrine of Santiago de Compostela. Joined to the mainland by a charming man-made bridge, the island has a 10th-century chapel, to which religious processions make their way on 24 June, 31 July and 29 August. The cliffs offer superb views of the sea.

◆ *The bridge to San Juan de Gaztelugatxe*

● Bermeo has the coast's largest fishing fleet

## BERMEO

The town of Bermeo is a fishing port, with the largest fleet in the region, and is very much a working town. Fishing boats of many colours can be seen in the harbour. As you might expect, the fish in the restaurants here is worth sampling. There is also a fishing museum in a converted building beside the harbour, which gives you a flavour of local life and work.

**Museo del Pescador** The museum displays the history of the reliance on the sea by the Basque people. Tales from whale-hunting and trading are related here, along with a claim to have reached the Americas long before Columbus. ⓐ Torronteroko enparantza 1 🕐 10.30–14.00, 16.00–19.00 Tues–Sat, 10.00–13.30 Sun, closed Mon ⓘ Admission charge

## MUNDAKA

Surfing is big in Mundaka – it is the best and most famous of all of Spain's Atlantic coast surfing destinations. It does have another claim to fame though: Mundaka was the first town in the region to be mentioned in recorded history. It's a base from which to explore the wildness of the Biscay coast and the town also boasts maze-like alleyways and a splendid promenade along its waterfront. A passenger ferry runs twice a day (June to September) to the white sands of Playa de Laida.

Accommodation options in Mundaka include:
**Mundaka ££** Family-run hotel with very friendly staff and comfortable rooms in a lovely old house. ⓐ C/Florentino Larrinaga 9 ① 946 876 700 Ⓦ www.hotelmundaka.com

🔵 *Gernika's historic* Casa de Juntas

## URDAIBAI

UNESCO designated Urdaibai a Biosphere Reserve in 1994. It covers 220 sq km (85 sq miles) of woods, marshland, beaches and cliffs, through which the river Oca runs. It is a beautiful and important refuge, and a breeding ground for thousands of migrating birds.
**Urdaibai Trust Information Centre** ❸ Palacio de Udetxea, Guernica-Lumo Road ❶ 946 257 125 ❿ www.urdaibai.org ❺ 09.30–13.30 Mon–Fri

## GERNIKA-LUMO

Gernika is now a byword for Franco's atrocities. The town that symbolised Basque democracy and tradition was devastated by the fascists, with the help of Hitler's Condor Legion and the Italian air force. Around 250 people were killed and hundreds injured in a bombing raid that lasted 3 hours on 27 April 1937, market day in Gernika and so the busiest day of the week. It was the first action of this kind in world history and acted as a prelude to World War II tactics.

The parliament building, or Casa de Juntas (❸ Pl. Allende Salazar), is open daily and is free of charge. English guided tours are available by appointment and there are also virtual tours in English. Monday is market day and numerous farmers go with their best products to sell at the Plaza del Mercado.
**Tourist office** ❸ C/Artekalea 8 ❶ 946 255 892 ❿ www.gernika-lumo.net ❹ turismo@gernika-lumo.net ❺ Daily

**Museo de la Paz** The Peace Museum provides a record of the 1937 bombing, using photographs, accounts and artwork. It's a pity that Picasso's famous painting hangs not here but in Madrid (see page 90). Two memorials can be found; one by Chillida – *Gure Aitaren Etxea*, or *Our Father's House* – and another by Henry Moore, entitled *Large*

*Figure in a Shelter.* ☎ 946 270 213 🅦 www.peacemuseumguernica.org
🄴 museoa@gernika-lumo.net 🕓 10.00–14.00, 16.00–19.00 Tues–Sat,
10.00–14.00 Sun, closed Mon ❗ Admission charge

The tourist office has details of places to stay. Try these options:
**Gernika Youth Hostel £** On the outskirts of town with great views
of the surrounding mountains. 🄰 C/Kortezubi bidea 9
☎ 944 650 775 🄴 gernika@suspergintza.net

**Akelarre ££** Nice, centrally situated hotel on a pedestrianised street.
🄰 C/Barrenkale 5 ☎ 946 270 197 🅦 www.hotelakelarre.com
🄴 akelarre@hotel-akelarre.com

**Hotel Gernika ££** Traditional Basque colonial-style hotel, built
in 1963 but with a modern interior, near the centre of the older
part of town. Accommodation is inexpensive but good quality.
🄰 C/Carlos Gangoiti 17 ☎ 946 250 350 🖷 946 255 874
🅦 www.hotel-gernika.com

## ELANTXOBE

A delightful Basque fishing village that has barely changed
with the passing of time. The village itself sits above the harbour,
joined by a picturesque cobbled street.

**Itsasmin ££** A nice hotel with restaurant. 🄰 C/Nagusia 32
☎ 946 276 174 🅦 www.itsasmin.com 🄴 info@itsasmin.com

## LEKEITIO

This elegant fishing town has two very good beaches: one near the
harbour, the other across the river to the east. The town is very

○ The village of Elantxobe spills down the hillside to the harbour

popular in summer, when local holidaymakers flood in from Bilbao.
The 16th-century Gothic church of Santa María is well worth a visit,
with its Flemish interior. Lekeitio has many bars and most have
food on offer. For more refined eating try the following:

**Kaia ££** Tasty seafood and great views of the harbour. ➊ Txatxo Kaia
5 ➊ 946 840 284 ➍ www.lekeitiokaia.com

**Meson Arropain ££** Great fresh seafood and fish. ➊ Iñigo Artieta
Etorbidea 5 ➊ 946 840 313

Accommodation can be thin on the ground in Lekeitio but try:
**Hotel Beita ££** Basic accommodation at reasonable prices.
➊ Av. Pascual Abaroa 25 ➊ 946 840 111 ➍ www.hotelbeitia.com

**Hostal Pinupe ££** Conveniently located next to the beach,
with basic rooms. ➊ Av. Pascual Abaroa 10 ➊ 946 842 984
➋ pinupehotela@euskalnet.net

● *The magnificent 19th-century façade of Bilbao's Estación Santander*

F-C DE SANTANDER A BILBAO

# PRACTICAL
information

# Directory

## GETTING THERE

### By air

Two airlines currently operate directly from the UK to Bilbao Airport. British Airways fly a twice-daily joint service from London Heathrow with Iberia, the Spanish national carrier; easyJet flies daily from London Stansted. Flight time is about two hours.

**British Airways** ☎ 0844 493 0787 Ⓦ www.britishairways.com

**easyJet** ☎ 0871 244 2366 Ⓦ www.easyjet.com

**Iberia** ☎ 902 400 500 Ⓦ www.iberia.com

Many people are aware that air travel emits $CO_2$, which contributes to climate change. You may be interested in the possibility of lessening the environmental impact of your flight through the charity **Climate Care** (Ⓦ www.jpmorganclimatecare.com), which offsets your $CO_2$ by funding environmental projects around the world.

### By rail

To reach Bilbao by rail from the UK you will need to make a few train changes along the way, so it will pay to carry as little luggage as possible. Frequent Eurostar services from London St Pancras International arrive at Paris Gare du Nord in about three hours. From there, you need to take the metro to Paris Montparnasse station to catch one of the four–five daily non-stop trains to Hendaye, the last station before the Spanish border; these are fast TGV services taking approximately five and a half hours.

From Hendaye, catch one of the regional Euskotren (Ⓦ www.euskotren.es) narrow-gauge services to San Sebastián (Donostia); there are trains every 30 minutes and the journey time is

37 minutes. Change again at San Sebastián for Bilbao; the hourly service takes around two and a half hours and arrives at Estación Atxuri in Bilbao; however, it's usually more convenient to get off at Bolueta in the suburbs and continue from there by metro to the city centre. An alternative is to take one of the main RENFE trains from Irun to Miranda de Ebro and change there for a RENFE train to Bilbao, arriving at Estación Abando (🅦 www.reufe.es). Up-to-date details of these and other Spanish train services can be found in the monthly *Thomas Cook European Rail Timetable*.

🔺 *One of Bilbao's distinctive trams*

**Eurostar** ☎ 0892 353 539 ⓦ www.eurostar.com
**Euskotren** ⓦ www.euskotren.es
**RENFE** ⓦ www.renfe.es
**Thomas Cook European Rail Timetable** ☎ (UK) 01733 416477;
ⓦ www.thomascookpublishing.com

## By road

Eurolines coaches leave from London Victoria and arrrive at
Termibús in Bilbao. Most involve a change of bus and up to a three-
hour wait in Paris. The overall journey time is about 22 hours.
**National Express** ⓦ www.nationalexpress.com

Bilbao is approximately 2,000 km (1,375 miles) by road from Calais,
mostly on (toll-paying) motorways. The shortest route is via Paris,
Orléans, Poitiers and Bordeaux, crossing the border near San Sebastián
and continuing on the A8 motorway to Bilbao.

Cars must carry a warning triangle, spare bulbs and a first-aid kit.
Headlamps must be adjusted for right-hand driving. Your car
insurance has to be valid for travel in Spain and you need a valid
national driving licence (an international licence is not necessary).

## By water

As well as the direct ferry route to Bilbao with P&O Ferries, Brittany
Ferries offers the alternative of sailing with your car to Santander,
further along the Basque coast, and driving on to Bilbao along the
A8 motorway, a distance of 103 km (64 miles).
**Brittany Ferries** Sailings from Portsmouth and Plymouth to
Santander. The crossing takes 24 hours and there are up to four
sailings per week depending on the time of year. ☎ 08712 440 744
ⓦ www.brittanyferries.co.uk

**P&O Ferries** Sailings from Portsmouth to Bilbao on a large ferry with accommodation for passengers and cars, cabins and leisure facilities. Departs 20.00 from Portsmouth on Tuesday and Saturday and returns from Bilbao at 12.30 on Monday and Thursday. The Spanish terminal is at Santurzi, which is 13 km (8 miles) from Bilbao.
📞 08716 645 645 🌐 www.poferries.com

## ENTRY FORMALITIES

Citizens of the UK, the Republic of Ireland, other EU countries, the USA, Canada, Australia and New Zealand are all permitted to enter Spain with a valid passport. A visa is required if the duration of the stay is more than 90 days. Visitors from South Africa need to ensure that they have a valid passport and visa, return or onward travel tickets and sufficient funds for their stay.

Visitors entering Spain are allowed to bring with them their personal effects, gifts, and tobacco and alcohol products for their personal consumption (up to reasonable limits). Sums of money over €6,000 must be declared.

Before travelling home you should check the duty-free allowances with the customs officers of your destination country. Under EU rules, no meat or dairy products (except commercial powdered milk for babies) may be brought into Spain.

## MONEY

Since 2002 the currency in Spain has been the euro. Easily distinguishable notes are available in denominations of 5, 10, 20, 50 and 100 euros, while coins worth 1, 2, 5, 10, 20 and 50 cents, as well as 1 and 2 euros, are widely used.

There are plenty of banks (*bancos*) and savings banks (*cajas de ahorros*) in the city, except in the winding streets of the old centre.

● *Bilbao's distinctive street signs tell you where you are*

Tourist hotspots such as Plaza Circular and the shopping streets are well served by banks and ATMs. The most convenient option is to obtain cash from one of the numerous ATMs attached to the bank buildings with your debit or credit card. Almost all ATMs in Bilbao accept international cards, but your bank is likely to charge a fee for withdrawals. All of the banks will accept traveller's cheques (with your passport), but will charge a commission. There are also bureaux de change in the same tourist areas as the banks, and while some of them may not charge commission, their exchange rate will usually be lower.

Credit cards are generally accepted in the city's hotels, shops and restaurants, but don't assume that smaller establishments and museums will take plastic. If in any doubt, ask before embarrassment occurs.

## HEALTH, SAFETY & CRIME

Bilbao's drinking water is declared safe by the government, but many people prefer to drink bottled water for taste reasons. Bear this in mind when waiters try to persuade you to drink bottled water in restaurants. The city's food should present no health risk to travellers.

Spain's public healthcare system is very good, and, thanks to a reciprocal agreement, citizens of the UK and other EU countries are entitled to free medical treatment following the presentation of a valid European Health Insurance Card (EHIC). An EHIC is not accepted by private medical practices in Spain and does not entitle holders to free dental treatment (except emergency extractions). Apply for your EHIC online at Ⓦ www.dh.gov.uk and allow at least a week to receive the card. It is standard practice in Spanish hospitals to request ID from patients, so make sure that you have your passport with you.

Remember that the EHIC is no substitute for personal medical insurance and will not cover repatriation for medical treatment. Nationals of non-EU countries should ensure that they have adequate medical cover before travelling.

Tourists in Bilbao are not often the victims of crime and it is a safe place to visit, but keep an eye on your valuables in busy areas, because pickpockets will always be on the lookout for an easy target. There are two police forces, but you will not encounter them often on the street; the **Policía Local** deal with minor matters, such as traffic offences, and wear a blue-and-white uniform, while the blue-uniformed **Policía Nacional** deal with weightier problems like drugs and terrorism. See Emergencies (page 152) for more details.

Basque Spain is generally safe, with lower levels of crime than the UK. The usual, sensible precautions are advised when travelling. ETA's ceasefire was re-established in September 2010, but terrorist threats from other directions are always a possibility here, as in all other parts of the world, so you should apply the same degree of caution (about unattended bags, for instance) as you would at home.

## OPENING HOURS

Shops and offices tend to be open between 09.30 and 13.30 or 14.30, with a two- to three-hour closure before reopening at 16.00, closing again at 20.00. Banking hours vary – most banks open Monday to Friday 09.00–14.00 and Saturdays 09.00–12.30. They are always closed on Sundays and public holidays.

## TOILETS

Public toilets (*servicios* or *aseos*) are increasing in number in northern Spain but are still not plentiful. In an emergency you can nip into a café or bar, but it is polite to patronise the establishment afterwards, even if you only buy a coffee. The standard of public facilities is not uniformly high but those in the major museums are generally fine.

## CHILDREN

Children are widely welcomed and warmly regarded by the family-oriented Basques, as with elsewhere in Spain. It is quite common to see children eating out with the rest of the family in restaurants even late at night (though tapas bars and clubs are not suitable for children). The kids may not be happy to tour round many museums or churches, but they'll love the *Puppy* sculpture at the Guggenheim, and a ride in the gondola of the Puente Colgante or the Artxanda

◯ Children of all ages love a puppet show

funicular is sure to appeal to the older ones. The beaches of San Sebastián and other parts of the Basque coast are ideal for families, of course. All but very young children will also love the quirkiness, the fireworks and the spontaneous fun of the region's many festivals, though take care to keep an eye on them in street crowds.

Other activities specifically laid on for children include:

- **Kafe Antzokia** This Basque-language cultural and music centre devotes Sunday afternoons to performances for young children, including clowns, puppet shows and children's theatre. During the day it is a restaurant with a menu, and at night a concert hall. ⓐ C/San Vicente 2 ⓣ 944 246 107 ⓦ www.kafeantzokia.com

- **Guggenheim Museum** Activities and workshops for children at weekends, which must be booked in advance. Free guided tours for families and children aged 6–12, 12.00–13.00 Sun. ⓐ Av. Abandoibarra 2 ⓣ 944 359 080

- **Gran Circo Mundial** During the Semana Grande festival in August the 'great world circus' comes to Bilbao and sets up in the Parque de Etxebarría.

- **Karpin Abentura** This environmentally aware theme park in Karrantza (50 km/30 miles west of Bilbao) has attractions including Iberian and European fauna, animated dinosaur shows, recreational areas, exhibitions and restaurants. ⓐ Biañez auzoa ⓣ 944 479 206 ⓦ www.karpinabentura.com ⓔ karpinabentura@karpinabentura.com

## COMMUNICATIONS

### Phone

Coin- and card-operated telephone booths can be found all over the city. Phone cards (*tarjeta telefónica*) can be purchased at tobacconists (*estancos*) and newsagents. Any phone booth marked *telefono internacional* can be used to make calls abroad; it is cheaper to call before 08.00 or after 22.00. To phone home, dial the access code 00, then your national code (44 for the UK, 353 Republic of Ireland, 1 USA or Canada, 61 Australia, 64 New Zealand, 27 South Africa) plus the area code (minus the first 0 in UK codes), and then the rest of the number.

For international operator assistance, dial 11888 for information on international calls.

The Bilbao and other Spanish numbers quoted in this book include the local area code, a three-digit number, followed by a six-digit number. Dial the full number for calls from within Spain. To call Spain from abroad, dial the international access code (00 in the UK, for instance), followed by 34, the code for Spain, and then the number as shown in this book. For Spanish directory enquiries, dial 11888.

### Post

Post offices (*correos*) are open 08.30–20.30 Mon–Fri and 09.00–13.00 Sat, but those times may vary, especially in the summer. The main post offices can be found at Alameda de Urquijo 19 and Alameda de Mazarredo 12 (🕒 09.00–14.00, 16.00–19.30 Mon–Fri, 09.00–14.00 Sat, 10.00–14.00 Sun).

Stamps (*sellos*) can also be bought in tobacconists. Postboxes are a bright yellow colour. Mail from Spain is usually reliable and postcards take about five days to reach the UK.

**Internet cafés**

Cybercafés in the city include:

**Antxi** ⓐ C/Luis Briñas 13

**Laser Centre** ⓐ C/Sendeja 5

## ELECTRICITY

In Spain the current is 225 AC, 220V, and plugs are the continental two-pin type. Visitors from the UK will need a three-pin adaptor; visitors from North America will need a transformer to adapt the voltage.

## TRAVELLERS WITH DISABILITIES

Only limited facilities are available for travellers with disabilities, though some accessible accommodation is provided. The Bilbao tourist office has information sheets for people with disabilities. RENFE, the state rail company, provides wheelchairs at stations.

Sources of UK advice for travellers with disabilities include:

**Disabled Persons Transport Advisory Committee**

ⓦ www.dptac.gov.uk/door-to-door

**Radar** ⓣ 0207 250 3222 ⓦ www.radar.org.uk

## TOURIST INFORMATION

**Bilbao Turismo Offices**

The city tourist authority maintains three helpful offices in the city:

**Ensanche** ⓐ Pl. Ensanche 11 ⓣ 944 795 760 ⓕ 944 795 761
ⓔ informacion@bilbaoturismo.bilbao.net ⓛ 09.00–14.00, 16.00–19.30 Mon–Fri, closed Sat & Sun

**Guggenheim** ⓐ Av. Abandoibarra 2 ⓛ 11.00–18.00 Tues–Fri, 11.00–19.00 Sat, 11.00–15.00 Sun & public holidays, closed Mon

**Old town** ⓐ Pl. Arriaga (behind the Teatro Arriaga) ⓛ 11.00–14.00, 17.00–19.30 Mon–Sat, 09.30–14.00 Sun & public holidays

Bilbao Turismo publishes an informative guide, called simply *Bilbao Guide*, every two months (available from the above addresses), which is especially good for information on the latest festivals, pop concerts and events in general.

## Websites

**Bilbao** The city's informative tourism website is at ⓦ www.bilbao.net
**Basque Country** Visit the tourism website for the Basque provinces of Bizkaia, Gipuzkoa and Araba. ⓦ www.basquecountry-tourism.com

## BACKGROUND READING

The 'Guggenheim effect', the story of how the imagination and vision behind the building of this iconic museum helped rescue the city's declining industrial economy, is described in *The Guggenheim Museum Bilbao: Transforming a City* by Georgene Poulakidas (High Interest Books). One of the best introductions to Basque culture, showing how extensively this small nation has contributed to European and world culture, is *The Basque History of the World: The Story of a Nation* by Mark Kurlansky (Walker & Co).

# Emergencies

## EMERGENCY NUMBERS
**Ambulance and all-purpose number for emergencies** ⓘ 112
**Police** ⓘ 091
**Fire service** ⓘ 112
**Emergencias Osakidetza** (Basque health service emergency number)
ⓘ 944 205 101

## MEDICAL SERVICES
In an emergency you should ask to be taken to the nearest *hospital de urgencias* or *hospital de la seguridad social*. Under Spanish law, any health organisation, public or private, is required to treat patients in an emergency situation, regardless of their insurance status. However, emergency may be defined as a question of life and death and the responsibility of deciding what constitutes an emergency rests with the nurse or doctor on call. Holders of EHIC cards (see page 145) are entitled to basic medical treatment in any case, but travel insurance with a high level of cover is still advisable, and essential for non-EU visitors.

The emergency medical services are extremely good. You should try to give the age of the patient and type of emergency if calling 112, so that the ambulance can have a doctor on board if necessary. Some useful words are *ataque cardiaco* (heart attack), *ambulancia* (ambulance) and *médico* (doctor). By law, taxis are obliged to transport medical emergencies to hospital when requested to do so.

If you are physically able, you can go to a hospital emergency or casualty department (*urgencias*) or a 24-hour public health clinic. The telephone numbers of first-aid stations are listed at the front of telephone directories and many are equipped with ambulances.

Most pharmacies list details of local clinics and hospitals where emergency medical treatment is available.

The following are the most central hospitals in the Bilbao area:

**Hospital de Basurto** ⓐ Av. Montevideo 18 ⓣ 944 006 000
**Hospital de Cruces** (Barakaldo) ⓐ Pl. Cruces ⓣ 946 006 000
**Hospital de Galdakao** (Galdakao) ⓐ Labeaga ⓣ 944 007 000
**Hospital Santa Marina** ⓐ Carretera de Santa Marina 41
ⓣ 944 006 900

If you need a doctor or medicine in a non-urgent situation and are unable to contact a doctor, ring the telephone information number ⓣ 11888 or a police station, either of whom will give you the telephone number of a doctor on call or the address of the pharmacy that is open. Usually the hotel you are staying at should be able to advise you. For a list of English-speaking doctors, the best advice can be obtained from local tourist offices or your embassy or consulate. For minor complaints you can visit a pharmacy (*farmacia*). Spanish pharmacies have qualified staff who can offer advice and help on complaints for which you would consult a doctor at home. Pharmacy opening hours are 09.00–13.00, 16.00–19.00, and there is always a pharmacy that operates outside those hours.

## EMBASSIES & CONSULATES

**Australian Embassy** ⓐ Torre Espacio, Paseo de la Castellana 259d, Madrid ⓣ 913 536 600 ⓦ www.embaustralia.es
**Canadian Embassy** ⓐ C/Nuñez de Balboa 35, Madrid ⓣ 914 233 250
**New Zealand Embassy** ⓐ C/Pinar 7, 3rd floor, Madrid ⓣ 915 230 226
**Republic of Ireland Consulate** ⓐ C/Elcano 5, 1st floor, Bilbao
ⓣ 944 230 414

**South African Consulate** ⓐ C/Las Mercedes 31, 4th floor, apt. 2, Las Arenas, Getxo, Bilbao ⓣ 944 641 124

**UK British Consulate** ⓐ Alameda Urquijo 2, 8th floor, Bilbao ⓣ 944 157 600

**US Embassy** ⓐ Torre Espacio, Paseo de la Castellana 259d, Madrid ⓣ 915 872 200 ⓦ www.embusa.es

---

### EMERGENCY PHRASES

**Help!** ¡Socorro! *¡Sawkoro!*
**Fire!** ¡Fuego! *¡Fwegoh!*
**Stop!** ¡Stop! *¡Stop!*

**Call an ambulance/a doctor/the police/the fire service!**
¡Llame a una ambulancia/un médico/la policía/a los bomberos!
*¡Lliame a oona anboolanthea/oon meydico/la poletheea/ a lohs bombehrohs!*

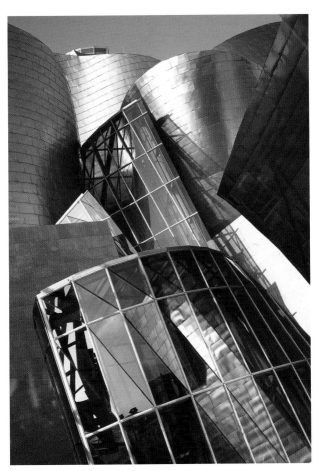

The Guggenheim Museum dominates the city of Bilbao

## ACKNOWLEDGEMENTS

The publishers would like to thank the following individuals and organisations for supplying their copyright photographs for this book: Wojtek Buss/World Pictures/Photoshot, page 65; Oscar Ruben Calero de Diago/BigStockPhoto.com, page 127; Ercilla Hotels, pages 42–3; Hemis/Photoshot, page 29; Graham Heywood/iStockphoto.com, page 7; Iratxe Ormatza Imatz, pages 32 & 70; Jarnogz/ Dreamstime.com, pages 25 & 38; Javiergil/Dreamstime.com, pages 5 & 87; Jorgefelix/Dreamstime.com, page 115; Liane Matrisch/Dreamstime.com, page 101; Fernando Pascullo/Wikimedia Commons, pages 52–3; Rainer Schmied, page 123; Luis Seco/iStockphoto.com, pages 92–3; StockExpert.com, pages 119 & 131; Telle/Wikimedia Commons, page 137; Álvaro Germán Vilela/Dreamstime.com, page 105; Jorge Vincente, page 141; Jarno Gonzalez Zarraonandia/iStockPhoto.com, pages 81 & 134; Neil Setchfield, all other pages.

Project editor: Tom Lee
Proofreaders: Caroline Hunt & Jan McCann
Layout: Paul Queripel

### Send your thoughts to
# books@thomascook.com

- Found a great bar, club, shop or must-see sight that we don't feature?
- Like to tip us off about any information that needs a little updating?
- Want to tell us what you love about this handy little guidebook and more importantly how we can make it even handier?

Then here's your chance to tell all! Send us ideas, discoveries and recommendations today and then look out for your valuable input in the next edition of this title.

Email the above address (stating the title) or write to: pocket guides Series Editor, Thomas Cook Publishing, PO Box 227, Coningsby Road, Peterborough PE3 8SB, UK.

## WHAT'S IN YOUR GUIDEBOOK?

**Independent authors** Impartial up-to-date information from our travel experts who meticulously source local knowledge.

**Experience** Thomas Cook's 165 years in the travel industry and guidebook publishing enriches every word with expertise you can trust.

**Travel know-how** Thomas Cook has thousands of staff working around the globe, all living and breathing travel.

**Editors** Travel-publishing professionals, pulling everything together to craft a perfect blend of words, pictures, maps and design.

**You, the traveller** We deliver a practical, no-nonsense approach to information, geared to how you really use it.

# Useful phrases

| English | Spanish | Approx pronunciation |
|---|---|---|
| **BASICS** | | |
| **Yes** | Sí | Si |
| **No** | No | Noh |
| **Please** | Por favor | Por fabor |
| **Thank you** | Gracias | Grathias |
| **Hello** | Hola | Ola |
| **Goodbye** | Adiós | Adios |
| **Excuse me** | Disculpe | Diskoolpeh |
| **Sorry** | Perdón | Pairdohn |
| **That's okay** | De acuerdo | Dey acwerdo |
| **I don't speak Spanish** | No hablo español | Noh ablo espanyol |
| **Do you speak English?** | ¿Habla Usted inglés? | ¿Abla oosteth eengless? |
| **Good morning** | Buenos días | Bwenos dee-as |
| **Good afternoon** | Buenas tardes | Bwenas tarrdess |
| **Good evening** | Buenas noches | Bwenas notchess |
| **Goodnight** | Buenas noches | Bwenas notchess |
| **My name is ...** | Me llamo ... | Meh yiamo ... |
| **NUMBERS** | | |
| **One** | Uno | Oono |
| **Two** | Dos | Dos |
| **Three** | Tres | Tres |
| **Four** | Cuatro | Cwatro |
| **Five** | Cinco | Thinco |
| **Six** | Seis | Seys |
| **Seven** | Siete | Seeyetey |
| **Eight** | Ocho | Ocho |
| **Nine** | Nueve | Nwebeyh |
| **Ten** | Diez | Deeyeth |
| **Twenty** | Veinte | Beintey |
| **Fifty** | Cincuenta | Thincwenta |
| **One hundred** | Cien | Thien |
| **SIGNS & NOTICES** | | |
| **Airport** | Aeropuerto | Aehropwerto |
| **Rail station** | Estación de trenes | Estathion de trenes |
| **Platform** | Vía | Via |
| **Toilets** | Servicios | Serbitheeos |
| **Ladies/Gentlemen** | Señoras/Caballeros | Senyoras/Kabayeros |